The 4 Simple Secrets
to Avoiding Life's BIG Financial

MESSTAKES

LEAVING A LEGACY
OF JOY AND HOPE
FOR PRESENT
AND FUTURE
GENERATIONS

The 4 Simple Secrets
to Avoiding Life's BIG Financial
MESSTAKES

REDISCOVERING
the Simple Secrets
to a Great Income,
Financial Independence and,
Most Importantly,
A GREAT LIFE!

Dr. Tom McCawley

KEYNOTE
PUBLISHING
A PART OF ADVANTAGE MEDIA GROUP

Published by Keynote Publishing, Charleston, South Carolina.
Member of Advantage Media Group.

KEYNOTE is a registered trademark and the Keynote colophon is a trademark of Advantage Media Group, Inc.

Printed in the United States of America.

ISBN: 978-1-59932-168-4
LCCN: 2009912134

This publication is designed to provide accurate and authoritative information in regard to the subject matter covered. It is sold with the understanding that the publisher is not engaged in rendering legal, accounting, or other professional services. If legal advice or other expert assistance is required, the services of a competent professional person should be sought.

Most Advantage Media Group titles are available at special quantity discounts for bulk purchases for sales promotions, premiums, fundraising, and educational use. Special versions or book excerpts can also be created to fit specific needs.

For more information, please write: Special Markets, Advantage Media Group, P.O. Box 272, Charleston, SC 29402 or call 1.866.775.1696.

Visit us online at **advantagefamily**.com

Required disclaimer:

The counsel published in this book is not a substitute for personalized legal or financial planning advice. Consult with your attorney, accountant or financial advisor before making any decisions.

50% of the profit from this book will be donated to enhancing dental education and reducing its cost.

**This book is dedicated as a legacy of joy
and hope to the ones I love:**

My wife, Brenda

My four sons, Tom, Paul, Dan and Mark

My brother Dan, his wife Carol and their family

My two daughters-in-law, Sigrid and Suzanne

My six grandchildren, Sam, Patrick,
Evelyn, Kincaid, Max and Zac

My practice partners Nick and my office team, my dental and
periodontal colleagues and my friends, all of whom are part of my
second family

And finally, this book is dedicated to all those who have struggled
with life and with finances, which is just about all of us!

Acknowledgements

WIND ON MY BACK!

Wow! I could write a book about my gratitude to all those who have been wind on my back.

The place to start is with my wife Brenda. Your spouse can be either wind on your back or a pit bull on your leg. My wife has been a huge wind on my back, sometimes maybe even a whip.

My four boys, Tom, Paul, Dan and Mark, have also been wind on my back by giving me purpose in my life and by becoming such wonderful human beings, despite my many *mess*takes* as a parent.

> *messtakes—mistakes, not learned from
> and repeated, create life's messes.
> Maybe Webster's will add this new
> word to their next edition?*

My mom, Delta, taught me to learn from others' *mess*takes and my dad, Byron, taught me what *mess*takes to avoid. I will quote my parents' wisdom and Solomon's Proverbs frequently in the text. This proverb certainly applies to me:

> *"Listen, my child, to what your father teaches you. Don't
> neglect your mother's teachings. What you learn from them
> will crown you with grace and clothe you with honor."*
> Proverbs 1:8, 9

My brother, Dan, has been a very strong wind on my back. It's a real joy to have him so close by. We talk frequently and he gives me wise counsel with a great sense of humor.

My partners in practice, Dr. Nick DeTure and my wonderful team of coworkers have been an incredible source of support and encouragement over many years. I couldn't have practiced periodontics or written this book without them and their support is appreciated beyond words.

Dr. Gerald Kramer, my mentor at Boston University's School of Graduate Dentistry, by his daily demonstration, taught me how to be excellent in all that I do. I'm so grateful for his mentorship and his many lessons.

Dr. L. D. Pankey, an outstanding dentist and philosopher in Miami, taught me early in my career the importance of balance and that being financially responsible is an acceptable and necessary part of being a great dentist and person.

Dr. Chuck Sorenson, a PhD in management with advanced training in psychology and a master's in divinity, taught me the new rules of management and the importance of mission, which changed my life.

A special thanks goes to my primary practice consultants, Bob and Marci Proebstle and Mary Ann Spears, for helping me manage my practice better and more profitably–the first critical step towards financial independence.

Paul Kraus, Bob Baker and David Souders, my financial planners, taught me most of what I know about money and helped me become financially independent, which also changed my life.

Greg Stanley, a dental consultant and speaker, taught me the importance of saving money outside the retirement plan as well as inside. He also taught me the importance of investing conservatively to not lose my money, which was very valuable the last few years.

Harvey Parker, PhD, my psychologist and friend, taught me how to use cognitive thinking to manage my thoughts. This changed the quality of my life in all areas and was very helpful in managing my thoughts about money, many of which are reflected in this book.

I owe a deep debt of gratitude to Yolanda Harris, my speaking and writing coach, for getting me started writing, encouraging me along the way and making this book ten times better than it would have been without her.

My editor and friends, Ann Nye West and her husband Jim, were extremely helpful in making my ideas more readable and organized. Their commitment and enthusiasm for this project was amazing and much appreciated.

A very special acknowledgment goes to my friend and cardiologist, Dr. Mike Chizner. As you will discover in reading this book, it would not have been possible without this incredibly caring, conscientious and competent man. In short, he saved my life. That's more than wind on my back. I would call it a hurricane. Words don't do justice to my gratitude!

Table of Contents

CHAPTER 4-THE THIRD SECRET: "DON'T LOSE!"

CHAPTER 5-THE FOURTH SECRET: "ENJOY!"

What Others Say About Why You Should Read This Book

"Over almost 20 years of advising families, I came to believe that a person's true character is ultimately revealed in the quality of their decision-making. Not all of us get it right the first time, but steady progress in our ability to choose between competing alternatives is essential to a life of significance and purpose. It's been my privilege, over the years, to observe Tom and Brenda McCawley's demonstrated ability to make difficult choices that result in enduring benefits to their family, their co-workers, their patients and their profession. I can readily attest that the principles Tom offers have been tested through their ongoing application in his own life. Dr. McCawley's book represents a distilling of years of personal and professional experience into a gift of immeasurable value to those with ears to hear."

Robert E. Baker
Principal Senior Financial Advisor,
Ronald Blue & Co., Orlando, Florida

"Tom McCawley looks like Clark Kent but when he grabs a microphone or a pen, he turns into Superman! He brings a unique combination of both being very practical and truly inspirational. I highly recommend his book to all who want more rewarding and fulfilled lives."

Michael A. Chizner, MD
Chief Medical Director, The Heart Center of Excellence,
author of the best-selling book in cardiology:
Clinical Cardiology Made Ridiculously Simple,
Fort Lauderdale, Florida

"Dr. Tom McCawley, a highly successful dental professional, has written an incredibly inspiring book that will prove to be invaluable to all readers interested in living a fulfilling life. He shows us that living well requires a focus on financial, spiritual, mental, physical and relationship health. Each is important to achieve, and Tom takes the reader on a very personal journey in his book to show us how to avoid mistakes that could lead to unhappiness. The lessons he teaches are delivered genuinely with warmth, humor, and wisdom and it is quite clear that Tom has found a formula for living a healthy, successful life. In addition, he shares it in an easily readable style. After knowing him and his family for over thirty years, I can readily attest that he 'walks his talk.'"

Harvey C. Parker, PhD
Clinical Psychologist, Plantation, Florida

"How successful could you be if you had virtually every obstruction to success removed—a roadmap, if you will, of how to navigate through a life that requires you to be a spouse, parent, business owner, professional, manager, employee, motivator and exceptional human being. Tom defines the term 'a man for others' better than any I have ever known. Tom goes to great efforts to translate his personal experiences into true learning opportunities to provide guidance in avoiding life's host of mistakes, or "*mess*takes," as he coins the term. Before I met Tom, I had as financially successful a practice as I could hope for, but I lacked balance and was quickly approaching burnout. As a fantastic teacher, mentor and friend, Tom has helped me prioritize my life and achieve the balance we all should seek to allow for a healthy and prosperous life. If you want *a highly successful life*, including financial peace of mind, read this book carefully, apply these lessons to your own life and pass them on to others."

Jason C. Stoner, DDS, MS
Columbus, Ohio

"It is not every day or even every month that you come across a great and exciting read, but I just did! This book by Dr. Tom McCawley is a must read! If you want a great income, financial independence and a great stress-free life, you must order this book today! I would like to thank Tom personally for all that he has done for dentistry!"

Howard Farran, DDS, MBA, MAGD
Founder and CEO of DentalTown.com,
Phoenix, Arizona

Preface

> This book was inspired by the following quote, which I keep on my desk at my office:
>
> *"The final test of a leader is that he leaves behind him in others the conviction and the will to carry on."*
> Walter Lippmann

"NEVER AGAIN!"

By **re**discovering timeless principles, my hope is that "never again" will many of an entire generation lose their way both financially and personally as happened over the last 30 years to my generation.

After probably the best economic times in the history of man, only a few people were able to achieve financial independence. Obviously, *mess*takes were made! In this book, I review practical examples of my own *mess*takes, and those of others, to help us— and those we love—learn from and avoid making these big financial *mess*takes again.

This is more than just a book about money and finances. It's also a book about avoiding the biggest financial *mess*take we could make—failing to integrate our pursuit of money into living a well balanced, fulfilling life.

Have you been burned by the claims of stockbrokers and real estate agents that "This time it's different"? This book *is* different from the thousands of other books on money and life management in that it reminds us that "The rules of life never change!" In fact, the more things change, the more they stay the same. The cycles of fear and greed, and feast and famine have gone on for thousands of years and will likely never change.

I call upon the 3,000-year-old wisdom of Solomon and Aesop's fables, along with the modern wisdom of Warren Buffett, Vanguard founder John Bogle and my own parents, to help us rediscover ancient wisdom and time-proven secrets to financial health and a fulfilled life.

Because I have written this book from my perspective as a dentist, the principles in this book will be especially helpful for professionals and business owners. The book, however, has a much broader purpose. It is meant to inspire all people, young and old, who struggle with finances and life (which is just about all of us). It is meant as a primer of basic principles that we can use and pass on as gifts of joy and hope to our children and grandchildren.

My goal is to make a contribution to as many people as possible by changing the way we now commonly define success as primarily being rich and famous. I propose a new definition of success that includes much more: encompassing spiritual, mental, physical and relationship health. I call this living *a highly successful life* and finishing well.

Instead of having to make the difficult choice between "your money or your life," this book will provide you with a step-by-step plan to help you to go for having it all—a great income, financial independence and, *most importantly,* a great life!

Before Reading This Book...

1. Consider *why* you are reading this book. Some say purpose is the most important element in life. The famous German philosopher Friedrich Nietzsche said, "He who has a why to live can bear almost any how." Viktor Frankl used this quote to help him survive three years in German concentration camps during World War II. My dad also used this philosophy to help him survive after being captured by the Germans during the Battle of the Bulge.

   For example, you might want to make more money because you want to make a bigger difference with your life. You might want to achieve financial independence to do and be whatever you want and to provide for your children's education. It is desirable to pursue objectives that are both meaningful and pleasurable. Look into your heart and examine why you want to improve your financial health and your life. This is your "why."

   _____

   _____

   _____

   _____

2. List your specific goals for improving your financial health and your life. This is your "how." Many say that goals are indispensable to a happy life. For example, goals might include learning how to earn more money, save more money, not lose your money and enjoy your money wisely. Be sure to write down your goals! When we write down our goals, we are ten times more likely to achieve them. It's

like magic! So fill in all the lines in the book as you read. It also helps if your goals are SMART—Specific, Measurable, Achievable, Relevant and with a Timeline. Try to add these criteria to each of your goals. If you can measure it, you can manage it! There is also a place in the back of the book for you to write down and summarize the ideas you want to implement.

Measurement always improves performance.
If you can't measure it, you can't manage it.

For example, if saving is one of your goals, consider writing down how much you will save each month, when you will start, and how much you would like to save by age 60. If you wish, brainstorm all the questions you would like to have answered about finances and living a fulfilled life. Write them down, then come back and see if this book provides the answers to your questions. Hopefully, most of your questions will be answered. If not, you could pursue the answers in the books listed in the bibliography or elsewhere.

List your goals here

_____

_____

_____

_____

_____

_____

_____

_____

Achieving financial health and living *a highly successful life* is a challenging, difficult and very high-level journey. Be gentle with yourself when you don't reach the highest level in all areas. Remember the Japanese proverb: "Fall down eight, get up nine." When you fail, be gracious with yourself and simply begin again. Doing the exercises in this book will enhance your learning and implementation.

This book was written as a contribution to everyone. But I'm painfully aware that for those without jobs, some of the financial information, unfortunately, will be difficult to implement. Apply what you can and learn for the future.

"Get all the advice and instruction you can so that you can be wise the rest of your life."
Proverbs 19:20

"You Should Be Dead!"

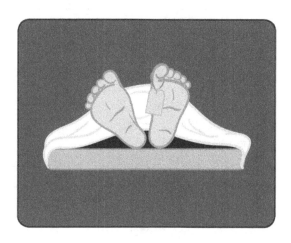

*"A wise person thinks much about death, while the fool
thinks only about having a good time now."*
Ecclesiastes 7:4

I opened my eyes in the hospital room to find my wife, Brenda, standing over me after what I thought was an unnecessary angiogram.

"You should be dead!" she said.

I had just dodged becoming another statistic of a surprising sudden death like the late host of NBC's "Meet the Press," Tim Russert. I, too, had a major blockage in "the widow maker," the left anterior descending coronary artery. Dr. Chizner, my cardiologist, said it was doubtful that with a 95% blockage I would make it through the weekend.

I had suffered an acute plaque rupture of a major coronary artery. This would have led to certain death without Dr. Chizner's insightful diagnosis and skillful intervention to open my blocked artery with a stent. Like most people, I had ignored my symptoms of fatigue and a dull pain below my sternum. Don't make this big *mess*take!

Brenda asked me, "If you had died today, would you have any regrets?" After thinking a moment, I said my only regret was not sharing all the information, *mess*takes and experiences of my life, including my near death experience, with my children, grandchildren, friends, colleagues and even the world so that they could learn from my *mess*takes and live more helpful, happier, healthier, wealthier and wiser financial and personal lives.

Brenda's brilliant question is one you might consider for yourself.

If you died today, would you have any regrets? If you would, what are they and what can you do during the rest of your life to eliminate them?

_____

_____

_____

_____

_____

_____

_____

That exchange was the genesis of what you're reading today. I feel I was given another chance to possibly make a difference by helping others to have more fulfilled lives.

In a sense, I feel like my mission is much like that of Jacob Marley's mission in Charles Dickens' beloved book, *A Christmas Carol*. When old miser Scrooge is visited by the ghost of his late partner, Jacob Marley, Marley warns Scrooge: "There is no space of regret that can make amends for one's life's opportunity misused! Oh! Such was I!" Scrooge argues: "But you were a good man of business, Jacob." "Business!" cries Marley. "Mankind was my business! The dealings of my trade were but a drop of water in the comprehensive ocean of my business! Hear me; I've come to warn you that you have yet a chance and hope of escaping this fate!"

Marley's words have a double meaning for me. In some ways they are a warning for me now, as they were for Scrooge, because I've sometimes focused too much on business and money. And, they have also awakened in me a calling to, like Marley, "Hear *me*; I've come to warn *you* that you have yet a chance and hope of escaping my fate, of regretting one's life's opportunity misused."

"The purpose of these proverbs is to teach
people wisdom and discipline."
Proverbs 1:2

Similar to Solomon's purpose for his proverbs, my hope is that the readers will hear me, gain wisdom from and also avoid some of my **mess**takes and the **mess**takes of others. Like Marley and so many of us, I certainly wish I had known earlier some of the things that I know now. It could have made my life better and more meaningful. By learning from my **mess**takes and following the wisdom of Solomon and others, perhaps we can escape the fate "of regretting one's life's opportunity misused."

Are you a Scrooge?
Will you heed
Marley's warning?

Decide for Yourself

Before I go further, I want to quote the words of the Dalai Lama to emphasize that:

"Although I speak from my own experience, I will not propose to you that my way is best. The decision is up to you!"

As you read this, remember I am only presenting my opinions! Although many were borrowed from others, as presented here, they are mine. Use them as you see fit. I understand that we all come from different backgrounds and that reasonable and responsible people can and will disagree with some of the opinions expressed in this book. If you already have a winning game, then stay with it.

And, as Mohandas Gandhi said, "I should love to satisfy all, if I possibly can; but in trying to satisfy all, I may be able to satisfy none… The best course is to satisfy one's own conscience and leave the world to form its own judgment, favorable or otherwise." I've satisfied my own conscience in writing this book; it's up to you to form your own judgment.

As you will see, I've made a lot of **mess**takes and lived real life problems. As an avid speed-reader, I have read hundreds of books and thousands of newspaper and magazine articles on how to deal with these problems—the very subjects we will be discussing in this book. I am presenting my philosophy of life. Yours is just as valid as mine. I am presenting one way that has worked pretty well for me and others I've observed. There are hundreds of ways to live *a highly successful life* and achieve financial health, but there are also thousands of ways to **mess** up!

MISTAKES
It could be that the purpose of your life is
only to serve as a warning to others.

My wife Brenda suggested that I use this poster in my book. (I'm not sure why.) I am in no way implying that I have it all together. I am a fellow traveler with you and I am still learning and making *mess*takes every day. Learn from my *mess*takes and let them serve as a warning to you. Evaluate my opinions and decide for yourself what is best for you! As Groucho Marx said, "Who are you going to believe, me or your eyes?"

MY GIFT OF LOVE

In writing this book, my purpose is to make the biggest possible contribution to the most people. In going this extra mile to use my time, learning, experience and empathy, I want to help more people create financial peace of mind, handle life's challenges more easily and live lives that are more meaningful, happier, healthier and loving.

One of the primary reasons I wrote this book was to help my children and grandchildren with their financial education. You can use this book in the same way and the exercises are included for you to modify as you wish for their education.

I want this book to help us avoid one of the really big financial *mess*takes we make in life: failing to integrate financial health effectively into our lives. We either overemphasize it to the exclusion of other areas like relationships, or underemphasize it so that we don't have the means to make a difference with our life. In either case, this big financial *mess*take causes making money to consume a disproportionate part of our life's mental and physical energy. I certainly made this *mess*take.

One of the premises of this book is that because we often spend money to feel better about ourselves, we need to work on our self-worth as well as our net worth. So this book is more than just a book about our financial health. There are thousands of books about financial health. And as hard as it may seem to believe, financial health is the easy part because there are time-tested ways to achieve it. And I will cover these in detail. I will also discuss what I consider the really hard part: understanding how our finances integrate into living what I call a well balanced *highly successful life* and thereby finishing well! Instead of having to make the sometimes difficult choice between your money or your life, this book aims to help you enjoy both—enough money *and* a fulfilling life!

I hope that by openly sharing the good, the bad and the ugly in my life journey, I can inspire others to realize that while virtually everyone has a bumpy ride on the road to financial peace of mind, these obstacles can be overcome in most cases. It seems to me that most books I read paint a rosier picture of life than most of us will experience. This can sometimes be discouraging especially when we hit roadblocks and think that others don't. I can assure you that almost everyone does.

As M. Scott Peck says in the first sentence of his book *The Road Less Traveled*, "Life is difficult. Once we truly see this truth, we transcend it."

He then adds, "Life is a series of problems. Do we want to moan about them or solve them? Do we want to teach our children to moan about them or to solve them?"

This book is about solving life's inevitable problems. It is relatively short because I believe that the so-called "secrets" are simple and don't need 500 pages to describe. In most areas of life, 90% of success is in the basics. What I have written is a synopsis of each area, a primer that you can use as a guide for yourself and for your children and grandchildren. Feel free to skip areas that don't specifically apply to you. You can and should get more explicit detail on each area from other authorities.

I've been told that writing this book is a useless endeavor since I am not a professional financial planner, there are over 7,000 books published in the financial and self-help area each year, and people aren't buying books anymore. Indeed, entire books have been written on some of the subjects that I discuss in one or two paragraphs. Many of these references are listed in the bibliography. Having said that, much of what you need to know is in this book. As my financial planner, Bob Baker, once told me, "Achieving financial health is not brain surgery."

I am motivated by the story of the young man on the beach throwing starfish back into the ocean. A man comes up to him and says, "There are millions of starfish washed up on the beaches along the East Coast. What possible difference could you make throwing a few back in the ocean?" The young man picks another starfish up, throws it back in the ocean and replies, "Made a difference for that one, didn't I?"

Like the young man helping the starfish, if I can help just a few people to have better and more fulfilled lives, the effort will have been worth it. As Mother Teresa said, "Don't do great things, do small things with love."

I hope you'll accept and benefit from my small gift of love.

Avoiding Life's Five Big *MESS*TAKES

With the 100th anniversary of the sinking of the Titanic approaching in 2012, I thought it appropriate to use drawings of a ship about to hit an iceberg on the cover. I also placed iceberg drawings in the book to illustrate that, like the Titanic which made at least five preventable *mess*takes which caused her sinking, we make at least five preventable financial and life *mess*takes which can cause us big problems.

Many of us are like Captain Ed Smith who said, "I cannot conceive of any disaster happening to this vessel. Modern shipbuilding has gone beyond that." Yet he made one of history's biggest *mess*takes by ignoring iceberg warnings and pushing the Titanic at full speed in an effort to set a new passage record for the Atlantic.

Likewise, in 2000 and 2008 many of us could not conceive of any circumstance where stock prices or home prices would drop so much. We ignored warnings that stocks and housing were over-priced and made potentially disastrous financial *mess*takes. Similar to Captain Smith, who planned to retire after the Titanic's maiden voyage, many of us have had our retirement plans seriously (but hopefully not fatally) disrupted by our *mess*takes.

I recently visited the Titanic Museum in Halifax, Nova Scotia. As the closest major port to the sinking, 306 bodies were brought there; 150 of the dead are buried there. I was reminded that like us, the Titanic's White Star Line made at least five big *mess*takes that resulted in the voyage not finishing well. There were not enough lifeboats and many were launched half full; the watertight compartments leaked; lookout William Fleet had no binoculars despite having requested them; the wireless radio operator ignored warnings about icebergs in the immediate vicinity; and finally, to reduce its weight and therefore save on coal, the ship was built with 1 inch thick steel instead of the recommended 1 ¼ inch steel.

> **AN ANCESTOR ON THE TITANIC?**
>
> Heightening my interest in the sinking of the Titanic was the discovery that a possible relative, Thomas W. McCawley, died in the sinking. His spelling of McCawley is unusual and the same as mine. The name Thomas is a common family name—mine, my son's, and my grandfather's, who would have been this man's contemporary. The Thomas W. McCawley of the Titanic was a gymnasium steward and, as part of the crew, reportedly kept to his post until nearly the end. He was probably an excellent swimmer because he told a survivor that he would not wear a life vest as it would hamper his swimming. Unfortunately, in 29° water he could only survive for a maximum of 15 minutes. He was 36 years old when he died.

This ultimately fatal final *mess*take caused the ship to break in half under stress and sink rapidly in two hours and 23 minutes with the loss of 1,504 lives. If the Titanic had stayed afloat another one hour and 10 minutes, the Carpathia would have arrived in time to rescue them.

We too make at least five big *mess*takes, most of which are preventable. We spend thousands of hours learning the technical aspects of our careers and almost no time learning how to manage our money and have a great life. We think these things will just happen naturally. Some people who haven't taken control of their finances and their life even look down on those who spend time studying how to have great financial health and lead highly successful lives.

Our five big *mess*takes are made in the five key areas that I consider part of living *a highly successful life*:

1. **Spiritual health**—When we have **no mission** to help others, we live a life with no meaning. This is the most critical health of all and empowers all the others.

2. **Mental health**—When we allow ourselves to use **victim thinking**, we become burned out and are not as happy as we could be. We must remember that we cannot become a victim unless we choose to be one!

3. **Physical health**—When we **neglect our physical health**, we end up with low energy, disabilities and an earlier death.

4. **Relationship health**—When we **see others as adversaries and undervalue relationships** rather than taking responsibility for their health, the result is all too frequently divorce, failed partnerships, infidelity, troubled children and few close friends. As one of my mentors, Dr. Chuck Sorenson points out, "Others are not our adversaries. They are struggling just like us. Blaming others is a self-attack. The more we blame, the worse we feel."

5. **Financial health**— We see **making money as an end in itself**, and don't manage our money well or enjoy it wisely.

The first part of the book will focus on solving the big *mess*takes we make in finances. Even before the recent recession, only a small percentage of people had accumulated enough money to retire comfortably. This occurred after probably the best economic times

(See boxed statistics.)

JUST HOW GOOD WERE THE PAST
25 YEARS ENDING DECEMBER 2007?

The Standard and Poor 500 stock index stood at 122.55 on January 1, 1982. Without reinvesting dividends it stood at 1478.49 on December 31, 2007. This is 12 times the 1982 amount with an annual return of 10½%. If you left the dividends in and reinvested them, your money went up an astounding 24 times the original amount for an annual return of 13.6%. During the same period, median home prices went from $62,200 to $227,700, nearly 3½ times the original amount, for an annual return of 5%. Median household income went up 2½ times in inflation-adjusted dollars from $20,171 to $50,233 in 2007. It may be a long time before we see another 25-year period like this.

in the history of the world. (See boxed statistics.) If you couldn't do it then, when could you do it?

You may be thinking that the *mess*takes made by the Titanic are a nice history lesson and these types of *mess*takes can't happen today, but just like we thought big banks and stock companies would never fail, they have. In 2008 and 2009, big banks like Wachovia and Washington Mutual and stock companies like Bear Stearns and Lehman Brothers did fail—and the MS Explorer hit an iceberg in the Antarctic on November 24, 2007 and sank! This was 95 years after the Titanic. Fortunately, because of the lessons learned from the Titanic *mess*takes, all aboard were saved. Coincidentally, this was of particular interest to my wife, my youngest son and me since we had been on the National Geographic ship Endeavor—the first ship to the rescue—on a trip to the Arctic fifteen months earlier.

The good news is we can and do learn from our *mess*takes. The Titanic disaster helped make today's ships much safer. As I sit on a cruise ship finishing this book, a lifeboat drill is being conducted for the crew. In addition to better crew training, ships are required to have more lifeboats than may be needed. An iceberg patrol today warns ships of potentially dangerous icebergs and watertight compartments are checked for leaks. Likewise, we can learn from our own personal *mess*takes.

Will you finish well?
Studies show that less than half of us will finish our lives well!

Many of us will end up with numerous regrets—broke, bitter, alone, disabled, depressed or even disgraced. What a tragedy to end up old and poor, or just as tragic—rich, regretful and alone, especially when these outcomes are preventable.

There are now relatively simple, time-tested, evidenced-based ways to avoid these big *mess*takes— to have a great income, be happier, healthier, wealthier, have better relationships and more meaning in our lives. I've spent a lifetime making big *mess*takes and uncovering these simple secrets. You'll see that most of them really are simple. But they're not really secrets; they've been known for thousands of years.

> ### YOUR LAST WORDS?
>
> Which would you rather have as your last words: The last words of rich and famous MGM movie mogul Louis Mayer, "It wasn't worth it;" or the words of baseball great Lou Gehrig who said as he was dying of amyotrophic lateral sclerosis, "Fans, you have been reading about the bad break I got. Yet today I consider myself the luckiest man on the face of the earth."

King Solomon has been called the wisest man who ever lived and after reviewing his proverbs closely, I must agree. I will quote him frequently. He said it best:

> *"There is nothing new under the sun. Is there anything of which it may be said, 'See, this is new? No! It has already been said in ancient times before us.'"*
>
> Ecclesiastes 1:10

And he said this 3,000 years ago! Three thousand years seems like a long time, but those years represent less than 1% of the 500,000 years that Homo sapiens have been living, learning and making *mess*takes on the planet! So even 3,000 years ago, Solomon learned from our ancestors the wisdom they had gained nearly a half a million years before him.

I will also quote some of the ancient wisdom of Aesop in the fables he wrote 2,500 years ago to further illustrate that we are **redis**covering the "simple secrets" man has known for thousands of years.

ARE THE OLD RULES OBSOLETE?

One of the challenges of figuring out what to do financially is the conflicting advice you will read and hear. Robert Kiyosaki, author of many books on finances including *Rich Dad, Poor Dad, Rich Dad's Guide to Investing* and *Increase Your Financial IQ*, expresses some provocative investment philosophies. Kiyosaki has a lot of excellent advice, especially when he points out in *Rich Dad Poor Dad* that your house is not an asset—it's a liability. If only we had listened better then.

I'm not so sure about his advice in his last book that "work hard, save money, get out of debt, live below your means, invest in a well-diversified portfolio of mutual funds is bad advice simply because it is obsolete advice." Maybe yes, maybe no. Kiyosaki would suggest that investing in real estate such as rental apartments or owning a large business is the way to become rich. Certainly, many have been successful with a strategy of investing in appreciating assets such as rental real estate. However, I owned rental apartments for a while and it was a happy day when I sold them. They were a real pain to maintain and manage. If this is your calling, go for it. But remember, leverage bites you if you get it wrong. This book is written for the person who has no time and no stomach for the big risk and big reward of these types of investments. It remains to be seen how Kiyosaki and those who follow his advice survive the recent real estate declines.

What Robert Kiyosaki calls bad and obsolete advice is what this book is about. I believe the problem is not that people followed this obsolete advice. I believe the big *mess*take many people made is that they didn't follow this timeless advice. This book is not about becoming super rich as you might if you follow Kiyosaki's advice. It's about reaching financial independence and having enough in our later years to live comfortably.

> *"Wealth from get-rich-quick schemes quickly*
> *disappears; wealth from hard work grows."*
> Proverbs 13:11

Do you think the rules have changed since Solomon? Again, reasonable people can differ. However, when anybody says to you that "this time it's different," watch out! It usually means the financial bubble is about to burst. Think about what happened in the last decade with stocks in 2000 and 2008 and housing in 2007. The absurd valuations were, just that, absurd. It was not different. Get professional advice, then you decide what works best for you.

The Fox and the Lion

We can turn to an Aesop fable to understand why these old familiar ideas are viewed as obsolete and the wise men who passed them along to us are viewed as no longer relevant. In this fable, a young fox that had never before seen a lion, met one in the forest. A single look was enough to send the fox scampering off. The second time the fox saw the lion he stopped to look at him for a moment before slinking away. But the third time, the fox went boldly up to the lion, slapped him on the back and said, "Hello there, old chap!"

The moral of the story is… We are so familiar with ancient principles that we tend to disregard them and view them as outdated. Remembering the fable of the fox and the lion (as they became familiar friends) can remind us to respect and take heed to not only what Aesop and Solomon have to say, but also to other familiar wisdom.

A New Definition for Success

Success: The attainment of wealth, fame, honors or the like.

Random House Unabridged Dictionary, 2006

Can this really be success? Is this all there is? This limited definition for success as just wealth, fame and honors concerned me for many years. I found an excellent summary of my thoughts in the book *Success Built to Last* by Porrus, Emory and Thompson. "The current definition of success is a potentially toxic prescription for your life and work. Nowhere do you find any reference to fulfillment, happiness, finding meaning and lasting relationships."

John Bogle, founder of the Vanguard mutual fund group, elaborated on this point in *Forbes* magazine. He calls it the silver lining around Wall Street's collapse. "We have had quite enough lionizing of the notion of 'success' as popularly defined by a certain kind of material wealth, fame and power."

I developed my own definition for success. I identified five major areas in which I made *mess*takes. These areas are essential to living what I believe is *a highly successful life*. They are spiritual health, mental health, physical health, relationship health and financial health. In my mind, one has to be successful in all five areas to live *a highly successful life* and finish well! This is obviously a high standard and one I struggle to meet. However, this is why I use the word "highly" in the definition.

One of Stephen Covey's seven habits in his groundbreaking book, *The Seven Habits of Highly Effective People*, is to "begin with the end in mind." It's also important to enjoy the process and the journey along this path. This is my goal for living my life each day and, in the end, my goal for describing my life as having lived well and ended well.

> **My definition of** *a highly successful life is*:
>
> *Going the extra mile to be wind on people's back through great relationships while feeling happy, satisfied and peaceful, healthy and energetic and financially free.*
>
> Dr. Tom McCawley

It's relatively easy to write a definition of *a highly successful life*. The real question is: "How do you do it?" What are the simple secrets, the steps to achieving this? That's what this book is about...

What is your definition of *a highly successful life?*

_____

_____

_____

_____

_____

_____

_____

_____

This book reviews the big *mess*takes we make in each area and the simple secrets to success that I rediscovered for each area. To prepare for such a daunting project, I synthesized and summarized what I learned in these areas and gave several lectures to my family and my colleagues in dentistry.

Many people have career and financial success, but by my definition are only partially successful. Warren Buffett and Bill Gates certainly appear to be successful in all these areas, in addition to being extraordinarily successful financially. But Howard Hughes and Leona Helmsley as well as many famous entertainment stars like Michael Jackson and Elvis Presley were, according to my definition, only partially successful at best.

If you have all the money in the world, yet have no purpose; if your physical health or your mental health is poor and/or if you have bad relationships, what good does it do you? Think of Howard Hughes sitting alone in a Las Vegas penthouse suite with only paid help around him; or Leona Helmsley, estranged from her family, living alone in a New York penthouse with her white Maltese dog, Trouble, leaving a $12 million trust fund for the dog and the bulk of her $5 billion estate to benefit dogs. Stories of this kind are not uncommon. How does that kind of life sound to you?

In addition, what good does money do you if you've lost your integrity? King Solomon said this very well.

> *"Better is the poor who walks in his integrity than*
> *one perverse in his ways though he be rich."*
> Proverbs 28:7

Think about Bernie Madoff and Allen Stanford, who allegedly stole roughly $25 billion between them. How do you think they felt, even when their schemes were working? How do you think they feel now? Madoff has been sentenced to 150 years in prison and even his sons won't visit him. His wife has to report all purchases over $100 to a court-appointed trustee. Stanford is now in jail facing charges. Did they finish well? Like Scrooge, they may have benefitted from a visit by Marley's ghost to warn them: You have yet a chance and hope of escaping this fate of one's life misused. Let us be sure to use our chance well.

I'm not saying that money is not important. Indeed it is important. I will simply be talking about keeping it in perspective. Money is the means we can use to make a difference with our lives. Its absence can cause untold misery in all the other areas of our lives if we let it. Even Mother Teresa needed money to do her good work, and so do we. A sign outside the Old North Church in Boston of "one, if by land, and two if by sea" fame says, "Even in the land of the free, we still need money for upkeep!"

Originally, I believed that financial health was the least important of the five healths that I had identified as part of *a highly successful life*—spiritual, mental, physical, relationship and financial. Until I learned that several of my dental colleagues and a group of orthopedic doctors in Fairfield, Connecticut with over 100 employees were among the many that lost most, if not all, of their pension plans from Bernie Madoff's $21 billion Ponzi scheme just as they neared retirement. One of my long-time patients broke into tears in my office because she had to put her dream house up for sale that morning because her husband, a retired airline pilot, had lost over half of his retirement. Other patients or their spouses were losing their jobs too, often through no fault of their own. I was hearing and reading more and more similar stories every day.

After seeing all the heartache and stress that financial *mess*takes were causing, I changed my mind about the importance of financial health. I now believe that financial health is as important as the other four areas of a successful life because, if it is not working, all the other areas usually suffer. It is hard to have a life mission if you have no money. It is much more difficult to be happy if you have no money. The stress of money problems often affects our health. My patient's husband had lost a lot of weight and she was very concerned about his health. Money problems are classic causes of relationship problems and even divorce.

After considering all this, my wife, Brenda, who has read *The Wall Street Journal* daily for ten years and reads each issue of *Forbes* and *Money* magazines cover to cover, told me she finds the level of financial education in this country appalling. She feels there is an urgent need for information and counsel—a simple primer—for financial health, and soon!

Being an obedient husband, I started writing...

CHAPTER ONE

The Four Simple "Secrets" to Avoiding Life's Big Financial *MESS*TAKES

"There is another serious problem I have seen in the world. Riches are sometimes hoarded to the harm of the saver, or they are put into risky investments that turn sour and everything is lost."
Solomon in Ecclesiastes 5:13

A modern sage said it another way:
"You only have to do a very few things right in your life so long as you don't do too many things wrong."
Warren Buffett

> **THE BIGGEST FINANCIAL *MESS*TAKE WE MAKE:**
> Focusing too much time and energy on making money and not enough on managing and spending it in a way that adds value to our life and others.

ALMOST A FATAL *MESS*TAKE!

Even with all my reading, coaching and thinking, I almost made a fatal *mess*take. As the late Paul Harvey would say, let me give you "the rest of the story" about my heart incident.

I was experiencing pain under my sternum for about ten days after exercise, but the pain went away with rest. Because I suffer from gastric reflux, I thought that's what was causing the pain. After all, I was in excellent shape, right at my ideal weight, eating right, exercising and playing tennis regularly. My last exercise echo stress test was only six months earlier, and when I asked my cardiologist, Dr. Chizner how I did, he said, "Perfect!"

However, when I felt the pain again after a Friday morning tennis game, I decided maybe another stress test might rule out any problem. When I called Dr. Chizner's office, I requested a new stress test sometime in the next month. His receptionist told me she needed the doctor's okay to book it, and since he wasn't in the office, she would have to call me back. Just then, Dr. Chizner, who was leaving town for a wedding in Orlando, called to check in with the office. He immediately called me on my cell phone and after listening carefully to my symptoms, asked me to come in the first thing Monday for the test. I told him I couldn't come in then, I had been gone for over two weeks, my appointment book was crammed full and I needed to see patients who had been waiting while I was gone. I was also concerned about losing more office production after being gone for two weeks.

He then insisted that I come by the office right then before he left and he would examine me. Again I declined, saying "I can't come in now; I'm in my tennis clothes." Lucky for me, Dr. Chizner persisted;

I did go in and because of his expert and conscientious care, avoided a fatal *mess*take. Due to Dr. Chizner's care, three years later, I can now state: "Reports of my death were greatly exaggerated!"

I nearly made a very stupid *mess*take that put convenience and finances ahead of my health. If I hadn't gone in and he hadn't seen me that Friday morning, it's likely that I would have had a fatal heart attack over the weekend during a planned tennis match. If that had happened, I would have lost more than just seeing my patients and Monday's production, I would have lost it all! How stupid!

Robert Kiyosaki points out this all too common *mess*take in *Rich Dad, Poor Dad.*

"We spend our health building our wealth, then we desperately spend our wealth to hang onto our remaining health." One of my mentors, famous dentist Dr. L. D. Pankey, said it another way: "The most important thing to save for your old age is yourself."

> **THE LIFE YOU SAVE MIGHT BE YOUR OWN!**
>
> I learned a lot from my near fatal *mess*take. Some of it might save your life. **Don't ignore symptoms like I did.** There's usually warning signs before cardiac arrest. The most common sign is a pressure feeling under the sternum like I had. It's not a sharp pain over the heart. **Don't think that it can't happen to you. 50% occur in people with no risk factors which included me.** Be sure that you, your family and friends know how to use an automated external defibrillator (AED). If a person is defibrillated within the first three minutes after cardiac arrest, the chance of survival is approximately 80%. It drops 10% per minute and is nearly 0% at 10 minutes. While waiting for the AED, call 911 and start hard and fast chest compressions.
>
> Make lifestyle changes **early**. Heart attacks can be reduced by almost 2/3 with a low-fat diet, weight control, exercise, not smoking and controlling blood pressure.

Hanging on a wall in my mother's kitchen was the following saying: "Learn from the mistakes of others: You can't live long enough to make them all yourself!"

GUM DISEASE:
"IT CAN KILL YOU!"

As a specialist treating gum diseases, I would be remiss if I didn't also mention that the bacteria infecting the gums can affect your health by spreading to the heart and other organs. In fact, the July 2009 issues of the *American Journal of Cardiology* and the *Journal of Periodontology* published an editors' consensus that recommended: "Patients with moderate to severe periodontitis should be informed that there may be an increased risk for cardiovascular disease associated with periodontitis." Whoopi Goldberg acknowledged this on the TV program "The View" when she said after her experience with periodontal disease, "It can kill you!"

It has also been found that those with high antibodies to a common periodontal disease pathogen had a 200% increase in their incidence of Alzheimer's disease.

To prevent gum disease and protect your health, I recommend regular professional cleanings and The **FBI** to control plaque with these four steps in order: **T**ongue cleaning, **F**lossing, **B**rushing and **I**rrigating with a diluted antiseptic mouthwash.

I would be equally remiss if I didn't tell you that **for more advanced problems, there is a breakthrough in treatment that I helped pioneer using a new specially designed Nd:YAG laser.** Like LASIK for eye surgery, minimally invasive laser surgery can now replace the blade and sutures for treating most forms of inflammatory gum disease. No longer does fear of the traditional blade surgery need to stand in the way of getting rid of your gum infection, saving your smile and possibly your life.

Be very careful climbing on ladders!

Although I've never fallen off a ladder, I know several people who have been injured severely and have heard of a few deaths. I have made many other *mess*takes along the way including working too much, investing in limited partnerships and in new technologies that lost money, taking very few vacations and, when I did, usually working while on them. I'll share more of them throughout the book.

DEFINING FINANCIAL FREEDOM, FINANCIAL INDEPENDENCE AND FINANCIAL PEACE OF MIND

No matter where you are, it's not too late to start working on financial freedom, financial independence and financial peace of mind. At age 40, I had very little money, three children, a new wife and a new mortgage. I was starting my periodontal practice over from scratch after dissolving a partnership and moving to a different area of town. By keeping my lifestyle under control, saving the excess money as my income grew and following the principles outlined in this book, my wife and I were able to achieve financial independence by age 60.

I define "financial freedom" as simply the ability to live on less money than we earn, or alternatively, make more money than we spend. Like many things, this is simple to understand, but not easy to execute. But it can be accomplished at any age.

I define "financial independence" as the ability to live your current spending lifestyle for at least 30 years before you run out of money based on a 3% annual rate of inflation and a 6% annual return on your money. A 6% return may seem unrealistic in the current market, but I'm really talking about a 3% return over inflation. I think over a 30-year time period, a 3% return over inflation is realistic. However, I recommend overshooting the mark with your savings, if possible, so that even if you don't realize this return, you will have enough.

With a higher level of financial independence your money would continue to increase for well beyond 30 years since your projected return of 6% would be well beyond your expenses. In this case, your money can potentially increase almost forever. We were able to achieve this higher level of financial independence at age 65 and still have enough to be on this path after the stock market losses in 2008. While this is a nice feeling, it is certainly not necessary, and may be too high a bar for most people to set.

Of course, one can obtain financial independence much more quickly by having fewer wants and a lower spending lifestyle. Achieving financial independence gives us the operational freedom to be and do whatever we want. Achieving financial independence usually takes many years of living with financial freedom. Like financial freedom, financial independence is relatively simple to attain, but definitely not easy. All you have to do is spend less than you make, save lots and not lose it.

Financial peace of mind for most of us mortals usually requires achieving both financial freedom and financial independence. Like financial freedom and financial independence, financial peace of mind is also simple, but very difficult to achieve, except for the most enlightened. Paradoxically, it is available at any time.

So how is your financial health, what *mess*takes have you made and where are you on the road to financial freedom, independence and peace of mind?

Think about where you are in making money, managing money and spending it in a way that adds value to your life and others. What is your current financial health? What's working and what would you like to improve?

Now that you have assessed where you are today, let's draw upon the financial wisdom from Solomon's proverbs and review the four simple secrets to avoiding life's big financial *mess*takes and enjoying financial independence and peace of mind.

AVOIDING THE BIG FINANCIAL *MESS*TAKES— THE FOUR SIMPLE "SECRETS"

Big Financial *MESS*TAKE #1: Not Earning Enough

Simple Secret #1:

Earn! Maximize your earning potential and net income.

Big Financial *MESS*TAKE #2: Spending It All

Simple Secret #2:

Save! Don't spend it all. Pay yourself first. Take the first five to 20 per cent of your net income and put it into a savings account for yourself.

Big Financial *MESS*TAKE #3: Losing It

Simple Secret #3:

Don't lose! Diversify to get rich slowly, stay happily married, have a well-considered tax plan and get insurance to protect yourself.

Big Financial *MESS*TAKE #4: Not Enjoying It Wisely

Simple Secret #4:

Enjoy! Invest it wisely on things that add value to your life and to others, such as family, travel, personal development, reasonable homes, hobbies you enjoy and helping others. Learn to appreciate however much or little you have and how to make the best of it.

I spent a lifetime discovering and developing these four secrets. I thought I was pretty smart until I discovered in the excellent financial newsletter, *Sound Mind Investing*, that Solomon had revealed these same four secrets 3,000 years ago. Obviously, this was not a new idea of mine!

Solomon the Wise

When I quote Solomon's proverbs or other religious passages, I am not necessarily referring to any specific religious faith. I am quoting them in the context of their timeless and inspired wisdom. With credit to Solomon for having these ideas a few years before I did, here are my four secrets:

"The rich rules over the poor and a borrower is servant to the lender."
Proverbs 22:7

This is my first secret: "Earn!" Solomon said it 3,000 years ago.

"There is precious treasure and oil in the dwelling of the wise, but a foolish man swallows it up."
Proverbs 21:20

This is my second secret: "Save!" Solomon said essentially the same thing, and again, I thought I was so smart.

"Divide your portion into seven or even to eight, for you do not know what misfortune may occur."
Ecclesiastes 11:2

This sounds a lot like Modern Portfolio Theory for which Harry Markowitz received the Nobel Prize in 1990. He pointed out that one could minimize risk by constructing a diversified portfolio that included many asset types, including some riskier types. Isn't this essentially what Solomon recommended—eight different asset classes? But to my knowledge, Solomon was never even nominated for the Nobel Prize.

This is my third secret: **"Don't lose!"** If only we all had remembered this one over the past decade with our investments in tech stocks, real estate and Bernie Madoff!

*"It's good for one to eat and to drink and to
enjoy the fruits of all his labor."*
Ecclesiastes 5:18

This is my fourth secret: **"Enjoy!"** Solomon knew 3,000 years ago that we should have fun with the fruits of our labor.

Do You Have a High IQ?

My mission, my "why," for writing this book is to offer as many people as possible ideas which, if implemented, will actually make a difference in their lives. My efforts and yours will  come to fruition only if you are able to implement the ideas offered. "IQ" as I define it is your *implementation quotient*—that is, how well you implement ideas to improve your life. Please implement those ideas you find valuable and pass them on to others. I've included exercises, questions and space for you to make notes to make implementation easier. As you read this book, you may want to place a star by the ideas you want to implement and/or want to pass on as your legacy to others. Write them down in the space provided at the end of each chapter and summarize them in the space provided at the end of the book.

"Many receive advice, few profit from it."
Publilius Syrus

**Which of these secrets would you like to implement
and when would you like to start?**

_____

_____

_____

_____

_____

_____

**Which ideas do you disagree with and/or what ideas of your own
would you like to add to pass on to others as part of your legacy?**

_____

_____

_____

_____

_____

_____

_____

_____

_____

CHAPTER TWO

The First Secret: "Earn!"

*"The plans of the diligent lead to profit as
surely as haste leads to poverty."*
Proverbs 21:5

FIVE STEPS TO EARNING LOTS

1. Choose a job or profession for which you have a passion and if possible, has a higher income. This is possible for younger people and occasionally still possible in later years.

2. Maximize your earning potential within your job category through training, good coaching, hard work and smart work. Model higher earners in your job category. Become very good, ideally the best, at what you do.

3. Let people know about your talent.

4. Be sure to focus on your net income after expenses rather than just gross income.

5. Don't quit your job too early (or too late).

The first step in maximizing your earning potential and net income is to choose a job or profession that you have a passion for and that has the potential for a higher income. One of my mentors, Dr. Chuck Sorensen says, "When you come to see your work as a mission to help others, you will never work a day in your life."

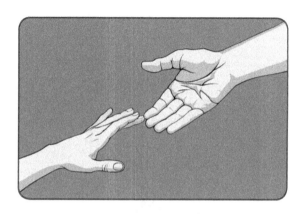

Passion and mission should come first. That's why writing this book was not work for me (except occasionally). It's also why my career as a periodontist, helping people save their smiles and remain free of gum infections, is not work. Superstar investor Jim Rogers gives this advice to his daughters in his book *A Gift to My Children*, "Where should a person start in order to be successful? Try as many things as you can, then pursue the one (or two, or three) about which you're passionate. The least happy people I know are those stuck in jobs they don't love."

In their terrific book, *Your Money or Your Life*, Vicki Robin and Joe Dominguez tell us, "Increase your income by valuing the life energy you invest in your job, exchanging it for the highest pay consistent with your health and integrity." I'm definitely not saying that earnings are your only criteria for choosing what you do. But I am saying that it is an important criterion that we should consider. For example, in my own case, I thought I wanted to go into journalism because I enjoyed my work as the associate editor of my high school yearbook. My father discouraged this career path since he felt that I would do better financially as a dentist and would enjoy that work as well. I think father knew best. Today, I'm doing well as a periodontist and living my mission to help others. And, as a coeditor of a newsletter that reaches 10,000 dentists and author of this book, I also got to be a journalist after all!

I know what some of you are thinking. You think that because I am a dentist, it is easy for me to talk about earning lots and achieving financial independence. It would probably surprise you to know that the largest financial advisory firm in the world for dentists,

> ### AVERAGE ANNUAL INCOMES
>
> The Bureau of Labor Statistics recently published average annual wages for various professions as of May 2008. This is a good starting point. For example, surgeons earn an average of $207,000 and general dentists, an average of $154,000. Nurses earn an average of $65,000, and paramedics, an average of $32,000. Lawyers earn an average of $125,000 and court reporters, an average of $52,000. Accountants earn an average of $66,000 and tax preparers, an average of $35,500. Each of these careers are related, but the extra education to move to a higher level position in that field increases income substantially. Keep this in mind as you plan your career. These average wages and incomes, in each category, can vary significantly either up or down depending on the ability of the practitioner.

Mercer Advisors, says that only 4% of dentists will retire comfortably and be able to maintain their standard of living. Like everyone else, even if we do make lots, we spend lots, lose lots and often don't enjoy it wisely. Dentists and other professionals need to apply these principles at least as much as anyone else and probably more so.

While I discuss professional jobs that require education, I want to emphasize that *all* jobs contribute to the lives of others by producing goods and services. The person who collects the garbage or delivers the mail makes as big a contribution to the world as does a neurosurgeon. All are essential to a fully functioning world.

It's also important to make sure that before you begin education in your chosen career, a job will be available for you when you finish your training. It's very unfortunate to spend a lot of money getting an education in a field with no jobs. My oldest son Tom began studying aerospace engineering just when jobs in this area began declining in the late 1980s. He changed his coursework to another area of interest, foreign affairs, and earned a master's degree. But again, it was a time when the Foreign Service was hiring very few people, so he was unable to get a job in this area either.

I'm not saying that pursuing a specific profession or job will necessarily guarantee a higher income in the future. As Yogi Berra said: "The future ain't what it used to be." The Internet and changing demographics will certainly impact most professions so pay close attention to these megatrends. Some say that in the future, many professions will be outsourced and much work will be done over the Internet. I'm simply suggesting that you examine the current and future job and economic situation and use potential earnings as one criterion for choosing your career, if financial health is important to you.

The second step to earning lots in whatever profession or job you have chosen is to maximize your earning potential within that job category. For example, if you choose to go into education out of your passion to help others, there are categories and jobs even within the relatively low-paying education field that will earn you much more than others. Getting a master's or doctorate degree will increase your earnings. At the highest level in education, some university presidents now earn more than $1 million per year, and many college coaches in football and basketball earn much more than that. Urban Meyer, the football coach at the University of Florida, earns $4 million per year and Billy Donovan, the basketball coach at UF, earns $3.5 million per year!

Choose a field for which you have a talent and passion. It should provide you a good income, if that is important to you. Then educate and train yourself for the jobs in your area that pay more. And finally, become very, very good, ideally the best, at what you do.

The reason passion is so important is that without it, we will never put in the time to be very, very good or the best at what we do. Michael Jordan became the best basketball player in the world because of his passion and hard work inspired by being cut from his high school basketball team. As pointed out by the authors in *Super Freakonomics,* deliberate practice does make perfect. "Deliberate practice has three key components: setting specific goals; obtaining immediate feedback; and concentrating as much on technique as on outcome." They say that "raw talent" is vastly overrated, it's lots of deliberate practice powered by passion that makes for excellence.

T. Harv Eker in his insightful book, *Secrets of the Millionaire Mind,* lists as his first wealth principle: "Your income can grow only to the extent you do!" He goes on to say: "Give me five minutes, and I can predict your financial future for the rest of your life by identifying your money and success blueprint!" Eker adds that earning lots "can be pretty damn hard." He has another excellent wealth principle: "If you're willing to do only what's easy, life will be hard. But if you're willing to do what's hard, life will be easy."

In his book, *Outliers,* Malcolm Gladwell presents several anecdotes and scientific studies to illustrate that preparation plays a much larger role in success than innate talent. He uses this to explain the success of Bill Gates, chess grandmaster Bobby Fischer and the Beatles. In fact, he points out that it takes 10,000 hours of practice over roughly ten years to be an elite practitioner in almost any area. The people at the very top don't work just harder or even much harder than everyone else. They work much, *much* harder. Eight thousand hours will make you very good, but 10,000 hours is the magic number for greatness.

> *"Lazy people are soon poor; hard workers get rich."*
> Proverbs 10:4

For earning lots, hard work is absolutely essential but it is not enough. Ditch diggers work hard for very modest incomes. Work *smarter* by choosing a higher earning job. Then look at the people in your job category or profession who are making more and model them. Most of them will be happy to share with you their secrets to financial success. Don't miss this opportunity, and remember to be very gracious with them for their time and knowledge. It's invaluable!

In my own case, I visited highly successful periodontists to observe how they maximized their income. I learned to be much more efficient and effective in delivering my service, and thus increased my income dramatically. I also increased my income with good coaching from consultants in my business. Hiring a good coach is one of the best investments you will ever make. This is true in all areas of your life.

The third step to earning a lot is marketing and sales. This is a critical skill. It's not enough to be very good if no one knows it. Don't hide your light under a bushel. Marketing yourself and your ideas is very important. Study marketing! Public speaking and writing is a good way to get your ideas known. Learn sales, which is essentially learning what people want by listening to them and then giving it to them.

The next step to earn lots is to be sure that you keep your eye on your *net* income, not just your gross income. In many businesses, it's very easy to have a very high *gross* income, but a very small *net* income after expenses and taxes. In my own profession, there are people keeping up to 60% of their gross income and, conversely, those keeping as little as ten or 15% of their gross income. This is a big difference and depends on what business you are in, but is sometimes the result of poor management of both productivity and the costs of doing business.

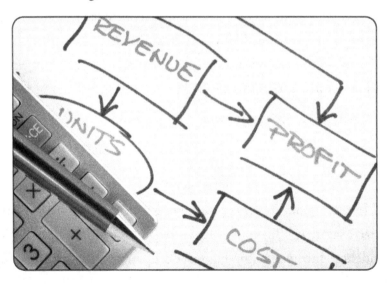

*So don't forget to pay attention to the bottom line—***PROFIT!**

The final step to earn lots is: Don't quit too early! In my experience, most of us will burn out several times in our careers, especially in our late 50s. Many people who thought they had enough money to retire have done so when they felt burned out. I thought about doing it! Fortunately, I was able to cut back my work considerably and do all the things I wanted to do like travel extensively and play tennis every day if I wished.

What often happens is that playing tennis or golf or fishing every day turns into a job itself and becomes a little boring if you can do it whenever you want. Many people even quit playing golf or tennis after several years in retirement. Besides that, our bodies won't hold up. I injured practically every muscle in my body as I began to play more tennis. I also traveled extensively through all seven continents and the Arctic. After more than a dozen flights from ten to 16 hours in length through time zone changes of seven to 11 hours, the thought of a long trip now almost makes me throw up, which I did a few times on these trips. Even my teenage son, Mark, spent most of a 16-hour flight back from India in the bathroom. As I write this, I'm on a seven-day cruise that starts in my hometown, Fort Lauderdale, and returns to Fort Lauderdale. What a pleasure!

My point is, be careful what you wish for.

BURNOUT

In their book, *Banishing Burnout*, Michael Leiter and Christina Maslach say that "Burnout is lost energy, lost enthusiasm and lost confidence. Burnout is the biggest occupational hazard of the 21st century."

Do you sometimes feel burned out?

But how does one avoid burnout? Having experienced burnout many times, and even depression at least three times for periods ranging from three to six months, I don't think most of us can. The key, at least for me, was to keep putting one foot in front of the other. As Woody Allen says, "Eighty percent of life is just showing up." Also, I didn't allow burnout to turn into crashing and burning. In other words, during these low periods I didn't make any major irreversible decisions. Almost always, these feelings will pass for most of us.

Another important key for me when I'm feeling burnout is to get back in touch with my mission to help others. This almost always works and my wife is very good at reminding me of this. When you're feeling burnout, go back to why you're doing what you're doing. It also helps to take a timeout, get some rest or take a vacation. As Vince Lombardi, the famous Green Bay Packers football coach, said, "Fatigue makes cowards of us all."

Another way that I handle burnout is by remembering some of the lessons I've learned from my travels. When feeling burned out,

I compare myself to those in India. I remember the crowding, the insane traffic, the poverty, the begging, the cows and the filth everywhere. With this image in my mind, I'm very thankful for being born in the USA. It puts almost all problems into perspective and helps to motivate me.

Another source of burnout is discovering yourself in your 50s with nothing to show for all the money you've worked so hard for over the course of your career. You've mostly spent it all on depreciating stuff. Fortunately, this didn't happen to me but I have many professional friends that it did happen to. This was one of the motivations for me writing this book. I was very distressed to see so many higher earning professionals end up with almost nothing to show for it in their late 50s. I hope the remainder of this book will help you avoid this unfortunate experience.

It can also be very beneficial to get psychological help, as I did during the especially difficult periods of my life, such as after my divorce from my first wife. We go to a physician for medical health problems, but often don't have the courage to go to a psychologist or psychiatrist for equally debilitating mental health problems. I learned to use cognitive thinking to manage my problems and

MANAGING MY OWN BURNOUT

Even as I was writing, reviewing and revising this material on burnout, I was feeling tired and burned out. I had given several different lectures over the previous two months and had been spending every spare moment writing this book. I really didn't want to go to work. I wanted to stay in bed and suck my thumb (just kidding about the thumb part). I applied the principles of just showing up, reviewing my mission, putting one foot in front of the other and keeping my mouth shut when I became irritated. It worked and then I followed my next suggestion and got some rest. I took a nap in the afternoon! It also worked!

messtakes. With diligence and constant reminders, this approach has worked well for me. I suggest looking into it. Most studies show better long-term results with cognitive therapy and cognitive thinking than with medication.

In her book, *Burnout: The Cost of Caring*, Christina Maslach says, "If all knowledge and advice about how to beat burnout could be summed up in one word, that word would be balance." Her basic message is that giving of yourself must be balanced with giving to yourself. She urges us to practice "detached concern," which is a healthy blend of compassion and objectivity.

It's been my experience in observing people in the health professions that those who care the most often are the ones that burn out first. We sometimes lose our most caring practitioners because they don't know how to manage burnout before they crash and burn. How unfortunate, when burnout is often manageable. While I want to emphasize the dangers of quitting too early, it's also important to know when it's time to quit our day jobs. The best advice I've heard on this is to ask your spouse or friends to tell you when it's time to quit.

Manage burnout. Don't crash and burn!

Today, I am extremely grateful that I did not quit my day job completely. It is what I recommend, if you can possibly do it. I do everything I want to do and I continue to work part-time. There are many benefits! It stimulates my mind and allows me to continue to make a difference in people's lives. It stimulates me socially in my relationships with my staff, patients and dental colleagues. It's good for my ego since I'm still a contributing member of society. It seems a shame to quit something at the top of your game after you finally learn how to do it very well.

I'm also happy to have the income after losing 25% of my retirement. Fortunately, I still have enough but as I will discuss later, you never know what will happen in the future. As Solomon in Proverbs 27:1 says, "Don't brag about tomorrow, since you don't know what the day will bring."

There are only four options to fix late career losses in a retirement portfolio. We can invest more aggressively, save more, count on less money in retirement or work

> ### A Cruel Punishment!
>
> The great psychologist Abraham Maslow said in his book *Maslow on Management*, "The typically implied notion in our society, perhaps throughout the world, is that labor is unpleasant by definition and that enjoying yourself means lying in the sun and doing nothing. But, to force people not to work is as cruel a punishment as could be devised!"

longer. Of these options, the most reliable way to reach our retirement savings goal is to work two or three years longer. By doing so we are able to save more, allow our money longer to grow, collect more Social Security by delaying retirement and have fewer years required for retirement income. Remember not to quit too early!

"If your boss is angry with you, don't quit! A quiet
spirit can overcome even great mistakes."
Ecclesiastes 10:4

What ideas would you like to implement to manage
burnout and not quit your career too early?

_____

_____

_____

_____

_____

_____

_____

_____

_____

_____

CHAPTER THREE

The Second Secret: "Save!"

"Take a lesson from the ants, you lazy bones. Learn from their ways and be wise! Even though they have no ruler to make them work, they labor hard all summer, gathering food for the winter."
Proverbs 6:6

Save lots—don't spend it all! Take the first five to 20% of your net income to pay yourself first. This age-old principle is not as easy as it sounds. Witness the last two decades during which the savings rate dropped to almost zero in 2008.

THE ANT AND THE GRASSHOPPER

One of the best illustrations of this principle is the 2,500 year-old Aesop's fable "The Ant and the Grasshopper." As we all remember, the ant worked all summer and saved food for the winter. The grasshopper lived the high life and made fun of the ant for working hard and saving food. When winter came, the ant had plenty of food and the grasshopper starved to death.

"Delaying gratification is the only decent way to live."
M. Scott Peck, *The Road Less Traveled*

Winter always comes, even in Florida where I live. Witness the severe recession of 2008, 2009 and perhaps beyond, and the fact that none of us can work forever. We eventually need and want to retire.

Perhaps the earliest written illustration of this principle comes in Genesis 41:29 in the story of Joseph. "Indeed the seven years of great plenty will come throughout all the land of Egypt; but after them seven years of famine will arise, and all the plenty will be forgotten and the famine will deplete the land." The Pharaoh authorized Joseph to collect one-fifth of the produce of Egypt in the seven plentiful years to keep as a reserve for the seven years of famine. When the famine came, there was plenty of food in Egypt.

Interestingly, the Egyptians were saving 20% of their income, the same amount recommended today. Also, notice that famine followed the years of plenty, which is not so different from what is happening to us in 2008 and 2009 after many years of plenty. This is not a new phenomenon, nor should it be unexpected since it was first recorded in Genesis about 3,800 years ago. These two stories illustrate well the importance of rediscovering the simple secrets to financial health. They have been known for thousands of years! And they demonstrate again my belief there is almost no new information or principles for living that haven't been known and written about long ago.

David Chilton's terrific financial self-help book, *The Wealthy Barber*, talks about saving painlessly:

Tom blurted out, "I know there's no painless way to save...no way, no how."

Roy asked, "Is there a painless way to save?"

"Sure is," said Mr. White (the wealthy barber). "Pay yourself first."

After agreeing that the ad hoc approach to saving doesn't work, and after explaining that the budgeting approach seldom works, Mr. White announced that the only real way to save is to "pay yourself first."

One study showed the urgency of starting to save no later than 35. At 35, if you make $60,000 per year and haven't started saving, you need to save 14.6% of income. Wait until age 55, and you need to sock away 32% of your income to have enough money for retirement at age 65.

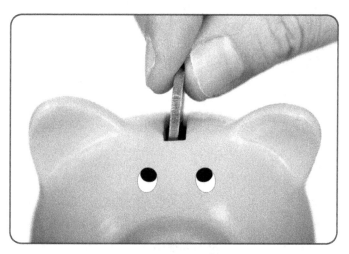

Start saving early!

Simply stated, if you don't develop the discipline to start saving early in your life, preferably by paying yourself first, you can never, and I mean never, have enough money to retire comfortably. The best way to do this is to pay yourself first with monthly automatic deposits directly from your bank account or paycheck to an investment account. Index funds, like those at Vanguard, are a good choice. The Balanced Index Fund, which has 60% in stocks and 40% in bonds, is a possibility if you are around age 40. Another possibility is Vanguard's Life Strategy funds, which range from 20 to 90% in stocks depending on your age and your risk tolerance. These funds have an expense ratio of .22%, which is almost 1% less than the average fund.

Einstein is reported to have said that one of the greatest miracles is the miracle of compound interest. It's remarkable how money accumulates. If you earned just 7.6% interest each year, your money will triple in 15 years.

Use the "Rule of 72" to estimate how long it will take your money to double: Divide 72 by the annual rate of return. For example, money compounded at 8% per year would take nine years to double.

Thanks to this power of compounding, someone who invests $400 per month at a 7% annual return for ten years from

> ### THE RICHEST MAN IN BABYLON
> George Clason summarized savings well in his classic book published first in 1926, *The Richest Man in Babylon*:
>
> "Now I shall tell thee the first remedy I learned to cure a lean purse. For every ten coins thou placest within thy purse take out for use but nine. Thy purse will start to fatten at once and its increasing weight will feel good in thy hand and bring satisfaction to thy soul. Debate this among yourselves. If any man proves it untrue, tell me upon the morrow when we shall meet again."

age 25 to age 34, and then stops saving will end up with more money [$602,559] than someone who saves the same amount at the same annual return for 30 years from age 35 to age 65 [$528,222]. The challenge is that few of us have the money to save at age 25. The point is, the earlier the better. We always think we will save later as our income grows, but our expenses also grow, so often it never happens. So start saving early.

To paraphrase Ben Franklin, a penny saved is actually better than a penny earned, since when you earn a penny you have to pay taxes on it before you can save it. That reduces its value from 20 to 50%, depending on your tax bracket. For example, $1,000 saved is equivalent to $1,500 earned, if you're in the top tax bracket.

If you borrow money from a bank or, worse yet, on a credit card, you are using the miracle of compound interest against yourself and you will have great difficulty getting ahead. Obviously, some borrowing is usually necessary for appreciating assets and quality of life expenses, such as a reasonable home and our own education. But even then, it is important to keep borrowing under control.

> ### EXCESS SPENDING
>
> "In many cases, excess spending is simply a means to cover over some emotional problem that is not being dealt with, or some emotional need that is not otherwise being met. In reality, those who are the biggest spenders are typically those who have the highest stress, not the greatest happiness."
>
> *The McGill Advisory*, February 2009

WHY MOST OF US DON'T SAVE

I think a big reason we don't save has to do with our ego, self-esteem and a belief we can buy happiness with more stuff. We think people will think more of us if we look wealthy. We also think more and bigger stuff will make us happier. It may, but only for a short time, and then we have to buy something else to get that same feeling. In happiness research, this is called being stuck on the "hedonic treadmill" of always needing more. By that I mean, we are like rats on a treadmill, continuing to run after more "things" and experiences to make us happy, never finding satisfaction and feelings of the contentment we seek. This behavior is also similar to that of lemmings, which just keep running until they plunge off a cliff to their death.

Madison Avenue geniuses play to our desire to feel better about ourselves through seductive advertising that suggests we need to constantly buy more to be happier and enjoy better lives. It can be difficult to resist the temptation. I recommend watching as few commercials as possible, and when you do, be aware of the clever psychological pull being used. Not only that, our country's leaders are constantly telling us we need to spend and consume to keep the economy strong. In the last few years, we can see where this philosophy has led our country and us!

"Those who love pleasure become poor; wine
and luxury are not the way to riches."
Proverbs 21:17

Buying stuff and accumulating money for ego or happiness is a big mirage. A dot-com multimillionaire that I met on an airplane told me that he had learned that people don't care a bit about your money unless you're going to give them some. Most of the apparent status that you get from money is from people that are getting money or something else from you, like free rides on your yacht. We see this all the time with the entourages around famous athletes and movie stars. A recent example, most of those people hanging around Michael Jackson were likely there because he was paying them.

I believe Morrie said it well in Mitch Album's book, *Tuesdays with Morrie*, "If you're trying to show off for the people at the top, forget it. They will look down at you anyhow. And if you're trying to show off for the people at the bottom, forget it. They will only envy you. Status will get you nowhere."

Solomon also commented on this:

"Then I observed that most people are motivated to success by their envy of their neighbors. But this too, is meaningless, like chasing the wind."
Ecclesiastes 4:4

Many times, if not most, if he looks like a millionaire, he's not! As they say in Texas, "Big hat, no cattle!"

Most of the people you envy are mortgaged up to the hilt, probably under water in the current economy and are living on borrowed money with credit cards that are maxed out. It's all a big façade. They get stuck on a treadmill of spending, can't get off and have to run faster, sometimes for their whole life. If you're on this treadmill, get off. It doesn't end well. Dave Ramsey says it succinctly and bluntly in his book, *The Total Money Makeover*. "Don't even consider keeping up with the Joneses, they're broke!"

The bottom line is: Be balance sheet wealthy, not appearance wealthy. Learn to distinguish between needs and wants. In my experience, you will be much happier, have much less stress in your life, and feel better about yourself for having the discipline to delay gratification when everybody else is spending.

Scott Peck emphasizes delaying gratification in his book *The Road Less Traveled*. "Delaying gratification is the process of scheduling the pain and pleasure of life to enhance the pleasure by experiencing the pain first and getting it over with. It is the only decent way to live." If only the grasshopper and many of us had read this before the winter of our severe 2008-2009 recession.

Don't Spend It All!

"The wise have wealth and luxury, but fools spend whatever they get."
Proverbs 21:20

Obviously, you can't save it if you have spent it all. So how do we spend it all? Basically, we develop a consumptive lifestyle and our spending goes up as fast or faster than our income. We develop expensive habits and hobbies like eating out, frequent vacations, country clubs, sports cars and boats. Some say, "I work so hard, I deserve it!" You do if you can afford it and you don't if you can't! There is no amount of money that one can't spend!

One of the most egregious examples of this "spend it all style" is former world heavyweight boxing champion Mike Tyson. He earned over $200 million in his career and ended bankrupt owing $20 million. Another example is NFL quarterback Michael Vick. He reportedly spent $17.7 million in two years, even though he was in jail for eight months of that time!

Ex-Miami Hurricane and Cleveland Browns' quarterback Bernie Kosar summed it up well when he said, "I'm great at making money. And, as we found out, I'm great at spending it. What I'm not great at is managing it." A recent *Sports Illustrated* article estimated that within two years of leaving football, an astounding 70% of players are either bankrupt or in financial distress over joblessness and divorce.

There are numerous stories like this among athletes, but I've also seen it many times among other high-earning professionals. Setting the bar really high for spenders is the late Michael Jackson who reportedly spent $20 to $30 million more than he earned for at least ten years, ending up an estimated $400 million in debt at his death! This record for spending and personal debt will be hard to top. His friend Al Malnik said of Jackson, "He will be richer in death than he was in life." Did he finish well?

One of the best ways to save is to control our lifestyle as our income goes up, and then to save most of the increased income. With my wife's great assistance, this worked well for me. In fact, it's essential that husband and wife agree on savings goals and on spending. My wife and I did this with the assistance of a fee-only certified financial planner. Our success in working with a knowledge-able third person is one of the primary reasons why I recommend a fee-only certified financial planner. We meet with our financial planner three times each year for about three hours and have done so for 20 years. We review our investments, budget and our spending and savings goals. We make minor modifications in our investments in terms of rebalancing, if indicated, or slight changes in the diversification of investments. My wife has tracked our expenses closely for 20 years so we know exactly how much money we spend each year.

If you hire a financial planner, make sure that person is certified. In the past few years, there are many people who have reinvented themselves as financial planners. Most of them make a commission on what they sell. It is nearly impossible to be unbiased in such a situation. For them, when they say fee only, it means their fees only come from what they sell you.

The most important financial goal for us is our savings goal. We set specific savings goals for each year, and my wife usually exceeds them. When you have specific savings goals, savings becomes more fun and more important than spending. Try this with your spouse. It sure worked well for us.

Fortunately for us, my wife has made herself very knowledgeable about finances. It enriches our relationship when she is a full participant and partner in our financial decisions. As she points out, many women ignore finances and leave it to their husbands. For these wives, the partnership is: You make it and I'll spend it. This can come back to haunt them, especially if they get divorced or their husbands die first, which is often the case. It can happen to husbands, too, if their wives are the major breadwinners.

It's important to have a reason for your savings to keep yourself motivated to save. We wanted to save enough to achieve financial independence so we could work because we wanted to, not because we had to. We also didn't want to be old and poor. Going to work because I want to adds a lot more joy to my work. I believe it also makes me more effective, because the monetary aspect of decisions is greatly diminished. Financial independence gives you the operational freedom to be and do what you want. This is a very nice feeling and a worthy goal in my opinion.

Be Frugal, Not Cheap

Obviously, we *need* to spend money on some things, and may *want* to spend money on others. Money is a means to an end, not an end in itself. I think it is important to be frugal with our money, but not cheap. By this I mean to shop carefully and get the best value we can. Today this is much easier with access to Internet sites such as Craig's List and eBay, and large volume retailers, such as Costco and Wal-Mart. For major expenditures, we almost always get three bids to be sure we're getting a fair price. Famous investor Bernard Baruch summed this up very well when asked the secret to his financial success: "I buy my straw hats in the fall." In other words, he buys when no one else does at reduced prices.

Vicki Robin and Joe Dominguez also have an excellent definition of frugal in their wonderful book, *Your Money or Your Life.* "Frugality is enjoying the virtue of getting good value for every minute of your life energy and from everything that you have the use of." It is a *mess*take to spend money on refurbishing your home, but not on your business or enhancing your job skills. Your business and job skills are what provide the money for the nice home.

And again we can turn to the ancient wisdom of Solomon.

*"Finish your outdoor work and get your fields
ready; after that, build your house."*
Proverbs 24:27

Fortunately, my wife listened to Solomon and understood this. She very graciously postponed spending on our house until our practice produced the income to afford it.

Another big *mess*take is to be pennywise and pound-foolish. It is not unusual for people to clip coupons to save pennies on groceries and drive way out of their way to buy gas at the best price, then turn around and buy a Porsche, a Prada purse and a large house without a thought about how much these cost.

We found ourselves being pennywise and pound-foolish when we went kayaking in the Antarctic. In the brochure, we saw beautiful pictures of people kayaking on a sunny day in calm waters with icebergs in the background. We thought this would be fun. When we got there, it turned out that all of the people on the trip were experienced kayakers. Some had been on the crew team in college and several had been training for months. When they asked me about my background, I said I had watched it on TV several times.

It was not sunny and the water was rough and obviously very cold. We had spent $600 each to go on several kayaking trips while on this cruise. Not wanting to lose our money, we went on the first kayaking trip. They warned us be very careful to avoid Leopard Seals which have been known to eat people. As fast as Brenda and I could paddle, we were still far behind the rest of the group and several times nearly capsized. We were wearing dry suits and were told that we could survive for 15 minutes in the 28° water. I had visions of us floating in the water frozen like the people on the Titanic. Brenda was in the back steering the kayak. After one experience of nearly capsizing, I gave her some negative feedback. She threatened to hit me with the paddle but thought better of it after realizing she needed me paddling to get back safely to the ship. By the time we got back, our marriage was tested and we were nearly frozen. Needless to say, we did not go out kayaking again. To avoid losing $1,800, we could have lost our lives. Now that would have been extremely pennywise and pound-foolish.

Kayaking in the Antarctic: It was windy and very cold!
Pennywise and pound-foolish!

LIKE ANOTHER PLANET

The Antarctic is amazing. It's like another planet. It's bigger than the USA including Alaska. It averages 50° colder than the Arctic and is 90% covered by ice that averages over one mile thick. The permanent human population is 0 for the entire continent. Without dry suits, the normal survival time in the water is about three minutes.

WHAT ABOUT BUYING A HOUSE?

One major way we overspend is buying a house that is much larger than we need: a McMansion. This is obvious now in the year 2009, but I have been saying this in my lectures for years: Your house is not a great invest-ment! Like a boat, your home is a money pit into which you keep pouring money. In calcu-lating the cost of a home, we don't include mortgage interest, taxes, insurance, maintenance and repairs. At 6.5% interest over a 30-year period, you will pay back in mortgage interest alone an amount that equals the purchase price, effectively doubling the cost of the house. And you can easily spend three times the purchase price of a house when you include these other costs. All those extra rooms have to be filled up with furniture and all those windows need curtains. All that extra space requires more utilities, repairs, etc.

So a $500,000 house may end up actually costing you $1,500,000! Yet, from 1994 through 2009, home prices produced an annualized return of only 4.7% a year and from 1982 until 2007 produced an annual return of only 5%. And we thought we made a lot of money on our houses!

Remember that buying a house as an investment or one you can't afford will not bring you joy. The number one cause of divorce is conflict over money. A big house is not necessarily a home. A house is just bricks and mortar. And it's not a home if you're never there because you have to work so much to pay for it.

A home is filled with love, warmth and joy. I know this too well. Early in my career, I made this big *mess*take. I had a house to die for but it did not make my first wife or me happy. She left me—and our three young sons— with only a day's notice. Obviously, there were many more things involved but the big house and the stress involved in its upkeep certainly contributed. I've seen too many people in my own neighborhood move into their supposed dream home and end up divorced within the first year!

"It is better to live alone in the corner of an attic than with a contentious wife (or husband) in a lovely home."
Proverbs 25:24

I suggest buying a home you can reasonably afford. I would even stretch a little on the first home. If you can still save for retirement and for your children's education, then spend the rest however you want, including a huge home. Just don't expect it to buy you more than short-term happiness. Your total home costs should not exceed 30% of your income at the very most and should preferably be at 25%. Even the government is now trying to get home costs down from an average of 38% of people's income to 31%. A time-honored and reliable guideline is to buy a house roughly twice your annual income. In some parts of the country, it may be impossible to buy a suitable house valued at two times your annual income, but keep this as a guideline.

Try to buy a home you can stay in a long time and be sure it is in a good location. Think about one of the richest men in the world, Warren Buffett, who has lived in the same modest home for 50 years. He says that "Enjoyment and utility should be the primary motives for purchasing a home not profit or refinance possibilities. The home purchased ought to fit the income of the purchaser." And we think we need a big home!

Moving frequently will increase your costs dramatically, especially if you live in Florida where your real estate taxes will increase each time you move. It also uses up a lot of your time and energy. Every time you move, the new home will require a lot of remodeling and new furniture to fit your tastes. This will be costly. I've lived in my house for almost 30 years and have seen houses turn over in our neighborhood several times. Each time the new owner spends a fortune remodeling, even if the new house was only remodeled a few years previously.

An especially big *mess*take I see people make is buying or building a very big house or building a very big new office while they are in their late 50s. This is often an ego statement, usually saddles them with lots of debt and makes retiring difficult. If it is done with mostly cash and is a life dream, then go for it.

On the following page is a photograph of a McMansion that I had built for my wife—you can see from the picture that even this did not buy her happiness!

Actually a picture of my wife Brenda, caught in a rare moment when she is not smiling, on a visit to the Neuschwanstein Castle in Bavaria.

LOCATION, LOCATION, LOCATION—
LIVE CLOSE TO WORK

We've all heard the three most important things about real estate are location, location and location. This may be a trite statement, but it is still very true. Never forget it. Houses in great locations hold their value better in down markets and appreciate more in up markets. One big **mess**take I almost made—and my wife saved me from making—was buying a house in the suburbs. Although it was much larger than the home we had been living in and would have provided our family more room, it would have required a 45-minute commute to my office. This would have been a **mess**take on two levels. Although the house we bought was a smaller house and needed fixing up, it was located on water in Fort Lauderdale and has appreciated much more than the larger suburban house. And, it's only about ten minutes from my office.

This is one aspect of location we often forget. If the breadwinner of the family has to make a long commute, it's very fatiguing. Even a

30-minute longer commute adds one, often stressful, hour to the workday. This adds 250 hours or over six more weeks a year to our work and time away from our family. In addition, there is the wear and tear on the car and the cost of gasoline. Don't kill or wear out the goose that lays the golden egg. It's the time and energy to produce the job earnings that provide the ability to buy the house. I've seen this happen several times. One dentist I knew burned out, quit his practice and went to work for the Veterans Administration. I think it was primarily because his commute of almost an hour wore him out. If at all possible, live close to work. I was reminded of this when a patient called me with a toothache on a holiday weekend. Living only ten minutes from my office, it was not a major inconvenience to meet her there and treat her so she would not be in pain over the long holiday weekend. What a relief for both of us!

The Hidden Cost of Cars

We can actually end up spending more money on cars than on homes over our lifetime. Most of us have at least two cars. If you have children, you may have three or four. When you compute the purchase price, loan or lease payment, the cost of depreciation, maintenance and gasoline, it's surprising how much money cars cost us. It is best to buy a car that is two years old after it has depreciated the most. It's best to pay cash and keep the car for five or more years. Having said this, I buy a new car because I'm concerned about repairs, but I keep it for six to eight years. It's rarely a good idea to lease a car.

Some people recommend using an auto broker to buy a car. If you do this, be sure there is a set fee and no commission to the broker. AAA automobile club and Consumers Report also provide auto buying services. I have not used these services but I think I will the next time I buy a car.

For the past few years, automobile dealers and other leasing companies were subsidizing leases and overestimating the residual value of cars. Leasing then sometimes made sense. Today, it is just another example of the excess borrowing of the past few years. We see how this worked out for the automobile companies and for the buyers. These times are likely over and buying a car with cash will again be the best route—as sound economic policy says it should be. If you must lease a car, don't lease it for more than three years. If you need a longer lease, it means you are buying too much car for your budget.

Watch out for ego when buying a car. I bought a Porsche when I was young. It was in the shop a lot and the repairs were enormous. You may not be able to completely avoid this ego pull. Just don't let it go crazy. Recently, when I was shopping for a new car, I almost fell for the ego pull of a Porsche again. Fortunately, my wife brought me back to my senses. I'm now happy I didn't fall for it. I recommend not buying a car on emotion, if at all possible. Give yourself some time. People who sell cars are geniuses at creating urgency and selling on emotion. Remember, the emotional thrill of buying will soon fade but the payments will keep going on and on, especially if you lease it.

The Cost of Children

Another way we spend a lot of money is on our children. Family planning is a personal decision. I have four boys. Originally, I only wanted two. But the last two boys have added tremendously to the joy and quality of my life. I could never put a monetary value on that and I definitely have no regrets that I had them. My point is to consider carefully the cost of children as part of your overall life planning.

Jim Rogers comments on this in his book *A Gift to My Children*, "Frankly, sometimes I even felt sorry for people who had kids. How did they have time or money for anything else? I was never going to do something so foolish. Boy was I wrong!"

Parenting is possibly the most important job on the planet. If everyone took this seriously and learned how to do it well, the world would work a lot better. Don't take this job lightly! I don't consider someone to be highly successful unless they have reasonably successful children and a healthy family life.

My family

"Many men can build a fortune, but very few can build a family."
J.S. Bryan

It's my belief that most education is the responsibility of the parent at home, not the schools. I feel that parents need to take responsibility for educating their children in reading, writing and math, and in passing on their values. We gave our sons homework assignments each weekend. The boys had to research a subject and write a report before they got their weekly allowance. On all our family trips, we were constantly playing educational games that expanded their knowledge, vocabulary and mathematical skills. We started reviewing and building vocabulary from a very early age so that by the time the boys took their SAT tests, they were fully ready and needed very little preparation.

> ### What Children Cost
>
> The US Department of Agriculture says that each child born in 2008 will cost a middle income family $221,000 ($292,000 when adjusted for inflation), after taxes, to raise through age 17. (For more specifics on your own situation, you can go to usda.gov for a Cost of Raising a Child Calculator.) In addition, we often think it's essential that they go to private schools from preschool through graduate school. These costs can easily exceed $500,000 per child in after-tax money. We would have to earn $750,000-$1 million per child to fund this!

A recent study by the National Association for College Admission Counseling found that SAT coaching by various companies increases scores by just 30 points. I don't think Andre Agassi started preparing for Wimbledon three months before the match. He started practicing for Wimbledon when he was six years old. I believe that if you educate your children at home, they will be ready for any school. I regard schools as an adjunct to their education and a way to build social skills. Don't blame the schools or the teachers if your child doesn't get a good education. Your child's education is primarily your job. This philosophy worked very well for me. Through it all, my wife and I kept our goal for the children in mind: that they become responsible, highly successful adults as they define it.

In my own case, my first three boys went to public schools all the way through high school. We chose to send our last son to a private middle school and high school because we felt the public school education in our area had deteriorated. Fortunately, by this time, our income had increased enough so that we could afford it. If private schools are unaffordable, maximize home education first, and then take advantage of honors and gifted programs and advanced placement courses in the public schools if your child qualifies.

Start saving for college when your children are very young.

State sponsored prepaid tuition plans are terrific. It's like investing in a tax-free municipal bond earning the state's college tuition inflation rate. College tuition rates have historically gone up faster than inflation (6% or more per year) and will probably accelerate in the future as states look for additional funding. Only a few states have these programs now, and they are starting to add restrictions, so investigate this option closely. In addition, consider 529 plans. The money you put in these plans is after-tax but the growth is tax-free. Look for a plan with low fees. For 2009 and 2010, the government has created the American Opportunity Tax Credit, which can be worth up to $2,500 per child depending on your income. Check this out with your accountant.

If you save money in children's custodial accounts, they will have control of the money after they reach 18. This is a concern for many people. I told my children that this money was for education only, and should they decide to spend it for anything else without my approval, it would cost them at least ten times the amount when they got their inheritance. This seemed to work and they used their money for education only. For a complete analysis of all of these college savings plans, go to savingforcollege.com and review the excellent book *Family Guide to College Savings* by Joseph Hurley.

Unless your child can get into an Ivy League or other elite school, like Stanford or Duke, I think it is far better for them to go to a relatively inexpensive, and usually less competitive, state school. In most states, and especially in my home state of Florida, the cost savings are enormous. It's also generally easier to get a higher grade point average at a less competitive state school.

This doesn't apply to some elite state schools like the University of California at Berkeley, Michigan, Virginia, the University of Florida and several others. In *Money* magazine, June, 2009, the University of Florida president said his school has become "ridiculously selective." These state schools have become extremely competitive and should be evaluated carefully.

The reason I recommend a less competitive school is that most, but not all, graduate schools look first at the grade point average and second at the school. A 3.6 grade point average from a state school or less competitive private school will give your child a better chance to get into most graduate schools than a 3.0 average from most elite and expensive private schools. Remember that at these highly competitive schools, virtually everyone in your child's class will have gotten straight A's in high school. Someone in the class will now have to make C's and D's. If it's your child, he or she probably won't get into a good graduate school if that is his or her goal.

It is equally important that you proactively pass on your values to your children. An often-unrecognized side effect of sending your children to an elite private school is their exposure to values that are different from yours. This, of course, may be desirable as part of their education. But it's not much fun, and definitely not what you want for your children, when they come home with values dramatically different from yours. This happened to a patient of mine and she wasn't very happy about it. I suggest preparing your children for this. My son, Dan, survived three years at Stanford Law School with his relatively conservative values intact. You have to be very hardy, confident and comfortable with your values to do this!

Another negative side effect of private education is exposure to a high spending consumptive lifestyle of peers. When most students have BMWs and go on ski trips over the holidays, it can be difficult to teach your child good financial values. One of our most important jobs is providing our children a good financial education. We need to start early so they can learn to manage their own money.

For college, we had saved a certain amount of money for each boy. We let them manage their own money and told them, when it ran out, they were on their own. This is the way my father managed the cost of nine years of college with me. This also worked well for our boys. Loaning money to children for college expenses is fine but be aware that it is often not paid back as their life expenses mount after graduation. Be prepared to handle this gracefully or it will create resentment in both parents and children.

Solomon also has some advice on friend and family loans:

"If you co-sign a loan for a friend, quick, get out of it if you possibly can! You placed yourself at your friend's mercy."
Proverbs 6:1

As my father did with me, we also advise our children not to count on any inheritance. We want them to be responsible for their own economic well-being. Of course, we would be pleased if it turns out that we do leave them some money. Our goal is to empower our children rather than enable them. Solomon again supplies some time-tested wisdom:

"An inheritance obtained early in life is not a blessing in the end."
Proverbs 20:21

One final point. College is not always the best choice for everybody. Trade schools and other careers can often be the best choice for some. This is especially so when you consider the sometimes enormous cost of a college education and the loss of income for several years while getting the education.

How I Almost Blew My Career Choice!

I learned the hard way about how going to a highly competitive school can create problems and that competition matters! After finishing as the top-ranked male in my small town high school class of 148, I started college at a highly competitive, private, Midwestern university and ended up with a 2.5 grade point average for the first year. In addition, after playing high school tennis on a team that won 80 straight matches, I couldn't make the college tennis team. I came down with mononucleosis that year and was also blackballed from the fraternity I wanted to join. Finally, I was on a fixed amount scholarship and they raised the tuition another 25% for the next year. Obviously, this was not a great experience.

Financially, it was already a stretch for my family to send me to this school, so, thankfully, the tuition increase encouraged me to transfer. If I had stayed there my chances of getting into dental school probably would have been poor. I transferred to a less competitive and less expensive small private university where I earned a 3.8 grade point average with the same amount or less effort, including an A in physics where my score on the final test was twice the next highest. This would have been nearly impossible at the previous school. This allowed me to get into dental school. I got into the fraternity of my choice, which was a blast, and I became captain of the tennis team. It truly was a great experience and taught me that, for most of us, competition does matter.

Based on my freshman academic performance, you may be thinking I was not smart enough to go to dental school. But after the first year of dental school and wonderful courses like neuroanatomy, I ranked eighth out of a class of approximately 100, and got A's both semesters in what was considered the toughest course, biochemistry. It is likely that transferring to a less competitive undergraduate school saved my career, so be careful where you go to school and where you send your kids to school.

Even with my own experience, I still didn't understand this completely and I sent my oldest son, Tom, to the Georgia Institute of Technology for engineering training. I learned later that Georgia Tech is noted for its rigorous academic environment and tough grading. Although my son was a National Merit Scholarship Finalist, at Georgia Tech he was only able to achieve a grade point average of 2.8. This, of course, was not entirely the school's fault. When he applied to law school, he could not get into the very top law schools. Because of a very high Law School Aptitude Test score, he did get into the University of Florida. In contrast to dentistry, it's very important in law what law school you go to. As a result, Tom had a harder time after graduation getting a good job. Fortunately, via family networking, he has a good job now, but it was a challenge complicated by attending a highly competitive undergraduate university with rigorous grading. Some schools have grade inflation and some schools don't. I suggest finding out ahead of time before it blows your career or your child's.

Sports—Show Me the Money

Another way we can blow our career is by putting all of our eggs in the sports career basket. As I have said before, money should not be the only consideration in choosing a career. There are many benefits to becoming very, very good at a sport. It's certainly great for one's self-esteem and fitness. I encouraged my children to play sports. It's certainly a lot better than playing video games or many other activities. If you or your child truly is an elite athlete then go for it. However, I suggest having a backup plan.

I've seen many people blow off other careers in the pursuit of being a professional athlete. The chances of making a career as a professional athlete are extremely small. Even if a major-league baseball team drafts you, only 1 in 1,000 ever play in even one game in the major leagues. In tennis, even if you are the best college player in the country, your chances of making a good living on the tennis tour are not good. Even if you do make it into professional sports, the average career is short because of injury and declining talent with age. In the National Football League, the average career is four years. Only a very few make enough money to live comfortably for the rest of their lives. In almost all professional sports, except golf, you are over the hill at about age 30. This leaves a lot of years to do something else.

The money saved by most college athletic scholarships is a mirage. Since college coaches are paid and retained almost entirely by their win-loss record, they are quite obviously primarily interested in the student's athletic performance. Most coaches' primary objective is just to keep the athlete in school. Especially in the men's major sports, the athlete's full time job in school becomes his sport, not getting an education. Most athletes simply pass their time in college in majors that will have little or no long-term economic value. If they don't make a lot of money in professional sports, they will have a big problem.

The money supposedly saved by the athletic scholarship also doesn't take into account the large amount of time and money spent on coaching, travel and equipment by both parents and children to develop an elite athlete. This can be a great bonding experience for the family but sometimes it's the parent's goal and not the child's. I've seen several cases where it burns out the child from playing the sport in adult life.

Certainly an athletic scholarship can be a good deal for families who could not otherwise afford a college education of their children. Female athletes seem to balance school and sports better so a scholarship for them can be terrific. But for many families who can afford college, I believe the blind pursuit of an athletic scholarship is a false economy.

EDUCATION COSTS MATTER

Harvard University

From my experiences, I also learned that unless you are very wealthy, cost matters. College tuition and fees have risen an astounding 439% since 1985. In comparison, the consumer price index has risen only 106% and the median family income 147% during the same time. It's good to remember that colleges don't compete on price. In fact, some college administrators fear that lowering their sticker prices will hurt their image. Be careful of getting caught up in the status seeking game of an expensive private education. Be certain that it's a good value.

If possible, borrow as little as possible for undergraduate education. Don't fall for the con that everyone borrows. Consider working to earn part of the cost. Times have changed, but I worked almost continuously for the nine years that I went to school. My children worked very little because we had saved for their education and they didn't need to. We also wanted them to focus on their grades to get into graduate school. In graduate school, they had no time to work.

Ideally, you want to start your career with as little debt as possible. However, depending on your situation, many times it's necessary and it's okay to borrow for education since this is an appreciating asset. Instead of thinking of the cost of a college education as an expense, you can reframe it as an investment. Getting a four-year college education can increase your income by as much as $1 million over a career, and possibly considerably more with a professional or graduate school education. Warren Buffett recently said, "Investing in yourself is the best investment you can make."

The average debt of dental students graduating from private dental schools now exceeds $225,000. One of my son's friends is borrowing $80,000 this year to cover the cost of one year of dental school. The US Department of Education reports that the federal student loan debt now exceeds $500 billion. The average undergraduate student graduates with $4,000 in credit card debt and $20,000 in student loans. This is certainly cause for concern as students, like many of their parents, borrow with little thought about the difficulty of

> ### A VERY USEFUL LIFE LESSON!
>
> One summer during college, I got a job laying quarter-mile rails for the Baltimore and Ohio Railroad Company. This was quite an experience. A few people in their 40s were still doing this work. Their skin looked like an alligator's and the foreman pushed them just as hard as they did us college kids. The working conditions reminded me of the pictures I had seen of the Chinese laborers laying rails in the 1800s. I had thought that those days were long gone. One day one of my friends collapsed from the heat and they just threw some water on him and kept working. When I got home at night, my whole body was covered with the creosote that they used to preserve the wooden ties. My pants would literally stand up on their own. I was so tired that I went to bed before 9:00 PM, a bedtime unheard of for a college student. This taught me that, compared to this, studying for physics and biochemistry was a piece of cake.

repayment. *Like the iceberg that was ignored by the Titanic,* this huge debt could be disastrous for the students' future finances, especially with the recent drop in incomes.

Recently, the government relaxed some of the rules for repayment and will forgive loans for some types of jobs, like teachers or those in the military. You will generally qualify for an adjusted

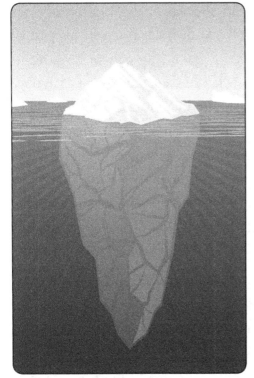

repayment schedule if you owe about as much in federal student loans as you make in a year. The Department of Education has more information at studentaid.ed.gov. Check this out if you have a student loan.

Don't overlook the option of going to the local community college for two years and then transferring to a four-year college. This can save a tremendous amount of money.

Education debt

To summarize, I believe attending less expensive, and usually less competitive, state schools first and then more elite expensive schools for graduate education is the best use of time and money. It also usually provides the best chance of getting into the graduate school of choice. Not all career paths and graduate departments are the same, so closely investigate your options to determine what the best path is. There is a *big financial iceberg* that's threatening to sink your retirement. In his book, *Pay for College Without Sacrificing Your Retirement*, Tim Higgins discusses the cost of a private school education.

"Let's look at a scenario for a family of four who will be sending two children off to elite private colleges. The total cost of eight years of private college could easily be more than $360,000 (eight years at $45,000 per year) after taxes. Those in the 28% tax bracket will have to earn $500,000 in order to meet this cost. If you are 50 now and plan to retire at 65, your current investments will be worth about four times what they are today, with an average return of 10% per year. For example, $30,000 saved today could be worth $120,000 at retirement. Even if you earn somewhat less than 10%, the growth in your retirement savings can be significant over a 15-year period. Keeping this in mind can motivate you to be more proactive in seeking out savings while figuring out how to pay for a child's college." Your kids will thank you when they're not supporting you in 25 years.

Furthermore, if your children go on to graduate school for an extra four or more years, like all four of mine did, it could cost another $333,000 each for a private graduate school education. If he decides to be a periodontist like his father, my youngest son may end up going to school seven more years after he finishes his undergraduate work. You can easily see that these costs can be enormous and easily sink our retirement plans. We started saving early for this and Mark spent very little for his undergraduate education. But, eventually, he will run out of money and will need to start borrowing if he studies the full seven years.

It's certainly okay to send your kids to private schools from preschool through graduate school, but the cost is exorbitant and not always worth it. Remember, it also often requires both parents to work more to pay for it. This will usually take time away from your children, which may actually be harmful to their development. Private schools are fine, if you can reasonably afford it, and still fund your retirement and your other needs. A little hardship is okay, but failing to adequately fund your retirement in order to pay for your child's private school education is not a good idea. You, and preferably your children, can borrow to pay for their education. But, as Higgins emphasized in his book, you can't borrow to fund your retirement!

Another consideration in the public versus private school decision is how long it takes to graduate. With budget cuts at most public universities and increased enrollments, it can be difficult to get the courses necessary to graduate in four years. In fact, one public university in our state has the nickname UCF—You Can't Finish. If it takes five to six years to graduate, the cost increases dramatically. Check out all aspects of the university *before* enrolling. Something as simple as parking can be a nightmare.

> ### THE BEST EDUCATION INVESTMENT
>
> I believe that spending the money on the last school you attend is the best investment. I went to the University of Illinois College of Dentistry and then to the more expensive Boston University for specialty training in periodontics. Because I attended a less expensive state school, I was able to start specialty training with no debt and cause much less financial stress on my parents and myself.
>
> Three of my sons went to state schools for undergraduate education and used their money later for more expensive graduate schools. One went to New York University graduate law school for tax and estate training after attending the University of Florida; one went to Stanford University Law School after attending the University of Florida, and my last son is a student at Nova Southeastern College of Dental Medicine after attending Florida State University.

Many private schools are offering great scholarships. If you can qualify for these, it might be a better value than a state school. Evaluate each option on its own merits. Your child can sometimes shorten the length of time necessary to graduate by taking advanced placement tests so that your child starts college with as many credits as possible. This depends on the specific college selected. All four of my boys did this and it helped tremendously.

As you can see from the previous discussion, the choice of college can have tremendous repercussions for both the child and the family. It should not be left to the child alone to make the decision. I've seen families make a big *mess*take by letting the child go to whatever college he or she wants and put a big financial burden on the family or, equally bad, go to a college that's not best for the child. It's the parent's responsibility to set some guidelines and help with the choice. The US News and World Report college issue each year is a great source of information. A terrific book on this is *College Admissions Together: It Takes a Family* by Stephen Goodman and Andrea Leiman. It does take a family to both raise children and help them make the best choice for college.

Finally, when thinking about education, remember the advice Robert Kiyosaki, in his *Guide to Investing*, received from his rich dad:

"School smarts are important but so are street smarts."

THE COST OF PETS

For many people the love and companionship they receive from their pets far exceeds the financial responsibilities and time commitment that they require. As with many items discussed in this book, finances are only one of the issues to be considered and usually not the most important one.

The Centers for Disease Control website points out the many health benefits of pets. Pets can decrease your blood pressure, cholesterol and feelings of loneliness. Pets can increase your opportunities for exercise and outdoor activities and opportunities for socialization. Discovery Health emphasizes how pets can alleviate loneliness and induce relaxation. It adds that "dog walkers have more fun."

However, it's important to our financial well-being that we consider their costs as well as their benefits. Puppies and kittens are cute for the first six months, but most of us do not realize the costs and time required to care for a pet. We are in an emotional place when we make the decision to buy a pet and do not realize that it is a ten year or more decision of time, money and energy.

My family has owned several pets over the years and certainly has enjoyed them. Having said that, one of the dogs had hip problems that cost us several thousand dollars to have repaired at a time when we had much less money. Every time we traveled, we either had to pay someone to watch the dog or pay a kennel. One person I know spent over $6,000 on veterinary bills for his dog. Another person I know spends probably one hour per day walking her dog and coming home at lunch to take the dog out.

Pets can use up a lot of our life's time, money and energy. That's okay, as long as we are aware and plan for the change they will make in our life, and we make a conscious decision that balances the many benefits against the costs.

While visiting the public market in Charleston, I saw a sign that was apparently there to encourage people to keep an eye on their children. It said: "Lost children will be given an espresso and a kitten." The espresso will last a few hours but the kitten will be with us for years!

This is the dog house I was put in for several hours by my wife after I didn't talk enough about the benefits of owning a pet in my first draft.

THE TWO-INCOME FAMILY DILEMMA

It is important to decide as a couple what you want your family income to be. In today's world of increased expenses, it may mean that both people want to work to support their household. It is also important, however, to consider the following: How could you live your life without increasing your expenses? Most people with a two-income household begin spending more, buy a bigger home and incur more debt. Soon, their two-income household becomes a "have to" rather than a choice. Think about how this has worked for others. Also think about what happens when you bring children into the equation. What if you or your spouse wants to stay home with your children? Could you live on one income?

I think families should try to live primarily on the income of one working spouse, usually the father. It is not unusual for the wife—rarely the husband—to want to stop working when they have children. Remember that, until recently, families have lived on one income rather happily. If expenses have become so high that both incomes are needed, this can create big problems for the family. Wouldn't it be great to have a choice?

WHAT ABOUT CREDIT CARDS?

Many people in this country are burdened with high interest credit card debt. In an October 13, 2008 Oprah television interview with Suze Orman, 225 of the 325 people in the audience had credit card debt. One woman, *an accountant*, had 23 credit cards and $79,588 in credit card debt. In addition, she had borrowed $33,000 from her 401(k) a year before in an attempt to reduce her credit card debt. Her monthly payment was over $1,800 for these debts alone.

One of my patients is a bankruptcy judge. After seeing hundreds of bankruptcies, his advice is to stay away from credit. Use it only as a rescue device when something unforeseen comes up. He sees people come in with five credit cards; each maxed out with $15,000. It means they have as much a $75,000 of credit card debt with 18% interest or more. This is almost impossible to handle.

A 2008 survey by student lender Sallie Mae found that the typical undergraduate student had four credit cards and the average balance was $3,173. This is not getting off to a good start financially! In recognition of this problem, the recent credit card reform law prohibits card issuers from visiting campuses to encourage students under the age of 21 to apply for credit cards. The law prohibits lenders from issuing cards to consumers under age 21, unless they can prove they can make the payments or their parent or guardian will cosign on the account.

It's really pretty simple, but not easy:
If you can't afford something, don't buy it!

Credit cards can be used for convenience but need to be paid off in full each month! Otherwise, the interest rates—which range from ten to 24% or more now—are exorbitant and will kill you financially. Paying off your bill on time each month is 35% of your credit score. Another 30% is based on how much of your available credit you are using (the lower the better). When you add the fees, such as late charges, it is unwise to use credit cards for borrowing and should be the first bill that we pay because of the high interest. Reduce your credit cards to just a few. Pay off the one with the highest interest first, then close it. To give you an example of how interest can add up, a loan of $150,000 at just 8% interest paid off over 30 years will cost more than $300,000 in interest alone. Credit card interest is usually much higher than 8%. In the banking world, they call the people who pay off their credit cards on time, deadbeats! Obviously this is because the banks don't make any money from these credit card users. In this case, I suggest being a deadbeat!

An example of how this interest and charges can mount up was revealed in testimony before Congress. One consumer testified that he got a Chase credit card in 2001 to help pay for wedding expenses. His limit was $3,000 and he charged $3,200. He said, "My wife and I wanted to show everyone a good time and have a memorable experience."

Eventually, Chase charged him $4,900 in interest, $1,100 in late fees and $1,500 in over limit fees although he went over his limit only three times. After making $6,300 in payments since 2001, he still owed $4,100!

In 2009, Congress passed a law to reduce some credit card abuses. Now we will at least know how long it would take to pay off our bill if we pay only the minimum payment, and how much interest would accumulate. For example, the minimum payment on a $1,000 purchase is typically $35. If we make only the minimum monthly payment, it would take 49 months to pay off the $1,000, and the interest alone would be $827.75, which would almost double the cost of the purchase. Before this law was passed, some people had no idea how much interest they were really paying, so this is an improvement.

And don't fall for interest-only payments for 12 months. The way companies make money on this program is that most people do not make their monthly payments on time and then have to pay interest charges back to the date of purchase at rates up to 29%. Again, if you can't afford something, don't buy it!

PAY OFF DEBT

One of the best ways to save money and earn a guaranteed return on it is to pay down non-tax-deductible debt, especially credit cards and car loans. The guaranteed return on your money ranges from ten to 20% or more. Paying off a 12% loan is the equivalent of earning a 20% return on a taxable investment, if you are in the 40% tax bracket, which you may be if you live in a state with an income tax. There is no investment like that anywhere, except from Bernie Madoff, and we know how that ended. I suggest paying off debt whenever you can, unless the interest rate is very low. Being debt free is very liberating. This was one of my wife and my first goals. After seeing the kind of return, which can be earned from paying off nondeductible debt, it almost makes me want to take on debt to get that return. Just kidding.

Mortgage debt is a little different since it is deductible on your income taxes and mortgage rates are very low now. If mortgage rates return to 7% or more, then I would consider paying off this debt also since it would represent a guaranteed 5% return after taxes on your money. You may or may not be able to exceed that return over the life of your mortgage. It's very nice on an emotional level to own your home free and clear, and when interest rates are higher, it provides a substantial guaranteed return on your money. If you pay off your mortgage in 15 years instead of 30 years, the savings can be substantial—often $100,000 to $200,000 or more, depending on the amount of your mortgage and your interest payment. Investigate paying off your mortgage and see if you can afford the extra payment involved. Another option is to take the 30-year mortgage and just make larger payments when you can afford it.

What ideas for saving do you want to implement and/or pass on to others as your legacy?

_____

_____

_____

_____

_____

_____

_____

_____

_____

_____

_____

_____

CHAPTER FOUR

The Third Secret: "Don't lose!"

*"Divide your portion into seven or even to eight, for
you do not know what misfortune may occur."*
Solomon in Ecclesiastes 11:2

A modern sage said it differently:

*"The first rule is not to lose it. The second
rule is not to forget the first rule."*
Warren Buffett

HOW WE LOSE IT!

The third and equally important part of achieving financial
freedom and security is not to lose the money that we earn and
save. Just as there is no amount of money we can't spend, there is no
amount of money we can't lose!

Nothing dramatizes this more than the scope of the Bernie
Madoff scandal, which totals a breathtaking $21 billion. I know

several people in their 60s who lost much of their retirement plan savings to Madoff's Ponzi scheme. They have little time to recover. This is very unfortunate and was mostly avoidable. Having said that, I wonder if a respected colleague had offered me the same investment opportunity if I would have participated? I have personally lost money by investing in two different new technologies and in a limited partnership apartment complex. I even considered investing more in a new toothbrush invention, but fortunately, my wife brought me to my senses. In his book, *How Harvard and Yale Beat the Market*, Matthew Tuttle points out that, "You can recover from mistakes in many areas of your life, but you may not be able to recover financially from an investment mistake." The reason for this is the cruel math of losses. If you lose 50% of your money, you will need a 100% return to recover your investment. This is because you have so few dollars working for you after a big loss.

William Barrett in the January 12, 2009 issue of *Forbes* magazine outlines seven *mess*takes we investors make. This is a wonderful opportunity to learn not only from the *mess*takes of others, but from our own, which is often the very best way to learn! I've added my personal comments in italics to his terrific list.

1. **The Reputation Ruse**–counting on the person's reputation when we make an investment instead of checking it out closely. *After all, Madoff was a former chairman of the board of directors for the NASDAQ. He should have read Solomon's Proverbs. It might have helped him.*

"It is better to be poor and honest than rich and crooked"
Proverbs 28:6

2. **The Affinity Fraud**–believing that because somebody is a member of our church, club or a friend, that they can therefore be trusted with our money. *This was also part of Madoff's scheme. He surely could be trusted not to steal money from friends, from his club and synagogue, couldn't he? To this list, I would also add family members. It is not uncommon for people to lose a lot of money investing with family members. Although it can be fraud, it is more often simply poor investing. But the money is lost nonetheless.*

3. **Falling for a Free Lunch**–falling for claims that are too good to be true. *Madoff's genius was offering very good returns regularly, but not extraordinary returns. In the words of Solomon:*

> *"A greedy person tries to get rich quick,*
> *but it only leads to poverty."*
> Proverbs 28:22

4. **Trusting Regulators to Protect Us**–The SEC rarely discovers things until after the fact. *Henry Markopolos wrote five different letters to the SEC from 1999 until 2006 pointing out problems with the Madoff investment scheme with minimal response. To this I would add, trusting our associations and organizations to protect us. They often receive large kickbacks for recommending investment programs and insurance. These need to be investigated just like any other investment. As a dentist, I had to find a place for the following advice from Solomon. I think it works well here.*

> *"Putting confidence in an unreliable person*
> *is like chewing with a toothache."*
> Proverbs 25:19

5. Putting All Our Eggs in One Basket–it pays to diversify for safety. *This is critical. In my defense, I think I would only have put part of my money with Madoff.*

Don't put all your eggs in one basket.

6. Falling for an Exclusive and Secretive Investment Idea– *If it's so good, why do they need our money? I'm still pretty upset that no one invited me to invest with Madoff. But I do feel better remembering Groucho Marx's words: "I wouldn't want to join any group that would want me as a member anyway."*

7. Fox Guarding the Henhouse–no third-party auditing of the results. *Be very careful that all of your investments are being watched over by competent third parties.*

Mark Twain summed all this up well when he said, "There are two times in a man's life that he should not speculate: when he can't afford it, and when he can." Sadly, he knew very well what he was talking about—he went bankrupt investing in new inventions for printing, which made him bitter at the end of his life. Unfortunately, he did not finish well.

The list of investment scams is endless and goes back to the beginning of time. It is not uncommon for some of us to spend more time planning our vacations or shopping for a car than researching and carefully planning our investments. Early in my career, I made this big *mess*take when I invested in an apartment complex that I had never seen located in another state. Predictably, I lost it all. We need to be very careful with our money. See the boxed story on how, ignoring my father's advice, I also lost money investing in oil wells. It is much easier to lose it than to earn it!

Some of us are addicted to the thrill of gambling with our money. In some cases, this may be genetic. Some people with certain genes get a bigger than average euphoric rush when they gamble. This rush is related to the release of dopamine in our brain, which makes us feel great. I think it is aptly named. We were given a prefrontal cortex to help us manage this rush and choose more wisely. We need to use it!

> ### MY DAD'S WISDOM
>
> My dad had another piece of wisdom to avoid losing money. "You can't beat a man at his own game." If someone is a professional at something, and you're not, watch out! For example, we invested in oil wells on our own family farm in southern Illinois. The oil company did hit oil, but charged us expenses and other fees equal to, and sometimes more than, the income from the oil. Finally, they were going to spend more money to water flood the wells to increase the production, and this would cost us yet more money. They offered to buy us out, and after several years of no return, we accepted. In just a few years, oil prices skyrocketed and the wells became very profitable for them. This was when I realized I didn't know oil!
>
> My dad also told me that if you have the money and the other person has the experience, when the deal is done, he will have the money and you will have the experience. That certainly applied to me in this oil investment, not to mention several others I have made.

We've all known people who lost their money through addictions to drugs or alcohol. If you have such an addiction, get help!

It never ends well. Witness the death of Michael Jackson and the previous deaths of Elvis Presley and Anna Nicole Smith and many others related to prescription drugs.

This is an excellent list of how we lose our money but there are other ways…

DIVORCE
"You Can't Be Serious!"

My initial thought was "You can't be serious!" the famous statement by John McEnroe, when my first wife returned from her high school reunion and told me that she was leaving me that night. Hardly believing my ears, I said, "We have three children, ages two, four and six, and you want to leave tonight?" I asked her if she could give me a day so that, at the very least, I could get some help to watch the kids. She agreed and left the following day.

As you might imagine, this was a difficult time for me. It led to my first significant depression. I got through it with the help of housekeepers, friends, family, psychological help and grit.

My first wife recently passed away. I paid for her funeral since neither she nor her husband could afford it. Over the years, I occasionally loaned her money, which she was never able to pay back.

Not long ago, her sister came to visit the boys. She asked me why I was always so kind to her sister when she had left me. I told her I thought she made a wise and courageous decision to leave the kids with me as it was in their best interest. Later, she shared with me that her sister had been diagnosed as bipolar.

I always believed that it was in my and my kid's best interest not to say anything bad about their mother and, for the most part, I didn't. At times, being human, I did feel some bitterness. I know I could have been a better husband. Her sister acknowledged it must have been very difficult for me with three kids, a busy practice and a life to live. Wanting to be gracious, I told her, "It wasn't too bad." "I know it had to be bad," she said. Tears came to my eyes and are coming again as I write this. I admitted to her, and even perhaps for the first time to myself, "It was brutal!"

My three sons—before my wife left.

By getting divorced, we can often lose much of our net worth and suffer considerable emotional pain. Despite my best efforts to put it back together, my relationship with my first wife was essentially unsalvageable. I definitely don't recommend staying in a truly bad relationship just for the money. Just be sure that you have done everything possible to save the relationship, and understand the financial consequences of a breakup.

A study by Jay Zagorsky in the *Journal of Sociology* reported on the financial status of 9,055 people from 1985 to 2000. Those who divorce lose, on average, three fourths of their personal net worth. I have a dentist friend whose divorce cost him $3.2 million after taxes over a 20-year period. He was forced into personal bankruptcy and is still working full-time at age 77. He calls his divorce a true "war of the roses." He suggests being very careful with whom you marry and if your marriage breaks up, get a very good attorney to defend you. He's an inspiration because, despite the fact that his ex-wife has most of his money, he made the best of it. He's happy, enjoying his work—and engaged to be married again.

These stories have led to a new definition for stock split, when your ex-spouse and their lawyer split your assets equally between themselves.

It's Okay to Sleep with Your Business Partner!

Your spouse is also your business partner. If you think not, wait until you dissolve the partnership. Therefore, it is very important that you consider this when you select a spouse. They can be a tremendous wind on your back, or they can be like a pit bull attached to your leg. King Solomon in 1,000 BC knew the value of a good wife or life partner when he said:

"Who can find a virtuous wife? For her worth is far above rubies.
She does him good and not evil all the days of her life."
Proverbs 31:10, 12

He doesn't mention that, with a bad spouse, you can end up with very few rubies, rubles or money of any kind.

In my first marriage, I made the big *mess*take of focusing on getting married instead of being married. By that I mean, we spent a lot of money on the wedding and honeymoon, leaving us in debt and starting our marriage off on the wrong foot financially. For my second marriage, we got married in our home and drove to Key West for a weekend honeymoon. We concentrated on *being* married instead of spending a lot of money on *getting* married. This worked out much better.

In his book, *Financially Ever After: The Couple's Guide to Managing Money*, Jeff Opdyke points out, "Couples today routinely enter marriage already laden with debt. This is akin to arriving on your wedding day with a negative dowry. Debt and money, it turns out, is a leading cause of family strife during marriage. This can undermine your marriage and cause the type of discord that can dissolve a marriage. We assume that we can change our partner to fit our own financial style. This rarely happens, so we need a neutral person such as a financial planner or accountant to mediate."

Even though my wife Brenda and I have similar attitudes about money, we still have significant disputes and have used our financial planner to mediate them. Sometimes, when we are in an enlightened mood, we simply accept our differences and agree to disagree. Marriage vows are usually for richer or for poorer, but many of us tend to forget that part of our vows when things get sticky financially. Opdyke suggests developing a family financial mission statement. "To live below our means, not to pursue material wants without the money to afford them, never to use emergency savings for consumer purchases, and to take on debt only when it benefits the family's long-term goals or needs." This is terrific advice!

Even though I was hurt emotionally and financially when my wife left me, it turned out to be one of the best things to happen to me. It encouraged me to grow, find a new, great, supportive wife and manage my finances. I was able to turn lemons into lemonade and a problem into an opportunity. I think this is the key to enlightened living.

Most people recover from one divorce, but two divorces or more can be fatal to one's finances. If it's a bad relationship, don't let money keep you in it, but again, do understand the financial cost.

"It is better to live alone in the desert than with a crabby, complaining wife (or husband)."
Proverbs 21:20

After Michael Jordan was cut from his high school basketball team as a sophomore, he said he never wanted to experience that again. So he worked very hard to prevent it. Like Michael Jordan, I was determined not to ever let another marriage end in divorce. So I learned everything I could about having a great relationship. My wife and I have attended the John Gottman relationship course in Seattle, Washington twice. I feel my relationship with my wife, Brenda, is the source of almost all the good things that can happen in my life, so it is worth a large investment of time, energy, thought and action. After 29 great years with her, so far it's working.

TAXES

Pay as little tax as you can legally! Never do anything illegal and report every single penny you earn. If you don't, your return could be four to ten. This is not the percentage return on your money, it's years in prison. Besides that, paying tax is part of our civic and ethical duty. If you don't report all your income, then you always have to worry about an audit. Ex-spouses and ex-employees are a major source of information for IRS fraud investigations. I heard of a dentist who caught a trusted employee embezzling. When he told her he was calling the police, she said "No, you aren't! If you do, my first call will be to the IRS because you haven't been reporting all your income." Needless to say, he didn't call the police. Don't make the big *mess*take of leaving yourself vulnerable to this kind of blackmail.

Don't allow the tax tail to wag the dog. If you pay 40% tax, it still leaves you 60% of your money to spend. It's not the taxes that you pay, it is what you have to save or spend that counts. Avoid clever tax evasion schemes. Almost all of them spell trouble and leave you with a large tax bill or even worse. I know of an ortho-dontist who went to prison after using one of these schemes. It may take years before the IRS catches up to you, but they usually do. Be sure the deal passes the smell test. If it smells fishy, it almost always is. Having said that, you want to maximize every deduction you can because your total taxes can be as much as 60%, if you add Social Security taxes and sales tax!

Work with a good accountant who understands the tax laws and what deductions are available and legal. Become knowledgeable yourself. Meet with your accountant at least twice a year before tax time. If you have one, run all major purchases by your accountant and financial planner before you make them. Afterwards is often too late to do any tax planning. I have done this a few times to my regret.

If you own your own business, one way to maximize deductions is to employ your wife and children in the business. They must perform legitimate services and the pay must be fair and reasonable for what they do. My boys started working at my office filing charts, cleaning and taking out the garbage when they were very young. I put the money they earned in a college account. I also paid them a modest allowance so they had some money to spend. Your family must be paid and that salary documented just like any other employee. My wife has been the bookkeeper and office manager for the office from the beginning, and, in this capacity, we get to go to dental meetings together. She attends most of the lectures with me and is a valued advisor.

There are numerous different types of 401(k), IRA and pension plans that allow us to put away money for retirement before taxes. The money continues to accumulate tax-free until you pull it out in retirement. Maximize these plans, especially if your company matches your contribution. If your company matches your 401(k), then this is an immediate 100% return on your money! Don't miss out on this. If you have extra money after your company match, then consider putting it into a Roth IRA. This money is after tax income that grows tax-free and is tax-free when you take it out.

You will have to pay ordinary income taxes on the amount you take out of your present IRA. This will reduce the amount of money working for you, so consider this move carefully before making it. Retirement plans can be very complex. Get an expert to help you with this so that you can maximize your benefits. Without careful planning, taxes can take a significant portion of our earnings and make it difficult to accumulate much money for retirement or other goals.

ESTATE PLANNING

The First Law of Financial Freedom in Suze Orman's excellent book, *The Nine Steps to Financial Freedom,* is people first, then money. She calls it being responsible to those you love. Part of finishing well, in my opinion and hers, is having a well-designed will and estate plan, and proper insurance to protect your family.

My son Paul, an estate-planning lawyer, sees disputes and squabbles among family members almost daily in his practice. He says most of these disputes are avoidable with careful planning and communication among the family while you're alive. Paul says that the first and most obvious step is just getting started on an estate plan. Because of the difficult and sometimes uncomfortable decisions involved, many people simply avoid the issue altogether, or do not give the issue sufficient consideration. Paul says there are two situations most likely to result in disputes: (1) a second marriage where there are children from the first marriage and (2) treating children unequally. In these situations, it is critical to carefully consider the ramifications of your estate plan and to be very specific with your desires in your will. If possible, you should also communicate your estate plan and the reasons behind your decisions, to your family so that your family isn't surprised by an unexpected situation following your death.

A well-known example of poor estate planning is that of Joe Robbie, the owner of the Miami Dolphins. When he died, his estate did not have sufficient liquidity to pay estate taxes and the family became embroiled in a bitter dispute. As a result, the team was sold for a much lower value than it was worth.

Another recent example is the estate of Eleanor Barzin, the daughter of Marjorie Merriwether Post who was the richest woman in the world at the time of her death in 1973. Eleanor died in 2006 leaving an estate valued at $74 million. Unfortunately she left multiple wills and trusts with no clear definition of how the estate was to be divided. Her only son and his daughter are fighting over the proceeds. With no end in sight to the litigation, lawyers' fees. taxes and administration expenses are expected to eat up almost all of the estate.

The biggest estate planning *mess*take of all is leaving no will. Do you want to have a say in where your money goes? How much of your estate do you want to leave to the lawyers? Reclusive billionaire Howard Hughes died in 1976 with no will and no children. Incredibly, more than 1,000 individuals claiming to be heirs and beneficiaries have come forward. Unfortunately for them, the last piece of real estate in the Hughes estate to be sold has now depreciated greatly and the corporate owner is in bankruptcy, so there may be little or nothing left of the estate as a final payment for anyone.

The emotional cost of a divided family is even worse than the financial cost. If you leave your family to fight over your estate, you definitely haven't finished well!

ASSET PROTECTION

Asset protection (i.e., protection from creditors) should also be considered as part of your estate plan. Most states protect certain assets from creditors. Your primary residence, annuities, retirement plans and life insurance cash surrender value are assets commonly protected. There are also ways to protect yourself without getting too exotic. You shouldn't overdo this, but you should pay attention. If you have significant assets, a minimum personal umbrella liability policy of several million dollars is essential to protect your assets. You don't want to lose all your assets in a lawsuit or bankruptcy, if it can be avoided.

You can also give away $26,000 per year per couple to reduce your taxable estate. However, you need to be very sure that your retirement needs are covered. That amount can be greater than you think.

INSURANCE

Another way we lose money is failing to have adequate insurance for major losses. It's very important to have good medical insurance that covers major expenses. In my opinion, it's a big *mess*take to be pennywise and pound-foolish here. Some people try to save on the small things, like co-pays and first dollar coverage on prescription drugs, etc. I believe in having a moderate deductible and making sure that you can choose your own physician for a serious illness, and that you will be covered for a major expense. One of my staff members was diagnosed with aplastic anemia. She needed the best specialty care, which cost almost $1 million. Part of the reason she is alive today, six years later, is because her insurance paid for her to get the best medical care available. If at all possible, don't make the mistake of going without medical insurance. Unexpected medical expenses were a major cause of 60% of personal bankruptcies in 2007, according to a study in the *American Journal of Medicine*. Three-fourths of those who declared bankruptcy had health insurance. If you have medical insurance be sure to check the exclusions and lifetime benefits.

Other insurance policies to consider are automobile liability, overall liability, flood insurance, disability insurance and overhead insurance if you have your own business, as well as life insurance for your family.

Don't even consider going without flood insurance if you are in an area that can flood like I am. Remember Murphy's Law. Anything bad that can happen will happen and at the worst possible moment. Those so-called 100-year floods seem to be happening every 25 years. If you go without any significant insurance for even a day, you expose yourself to Murphy.

> ### MURPHY'S LAW
>
> One of my sons made the big *mess*take of driving from Florida back to school in California without automobile insurance. He was going to get it out there because it was cheaper. Of course, he had an accident, which totaled his relatively new car. Fortunately, he was not injured. He called us and said he needed a check for $40,000 right away to pay for the old car and buy a new car in Las Vegas so he could finish the trip. Being irritable parents, we were not very happy when we found out that he did not have any insurance. We loaned him the money to pay for the old car and made him lease a new car. I know of another friend who was without automobile insurance for just one day and had an accident. Don't expose yourself to Murphy's Law.

I've known many people who had to stop work early because they became disabled. Some of them were in their 30s. I know people who say that they won't delay gratification and save now, they will just keep working. However, many times health issues make this impossible.

The May 1, 2009, *Morbidity and Mortality Weekly Report* by the Centers for Disease Control reported that 24% of the people in the United States aged 45 to 64 years old are disabled, and 52% of those 65 years or older are disabled. Most of them probably made the big *mess*take of not having adequate disability insurance. The CDC report cited arthritis as the number one cause of disability, followed by back problems and then heart disease. Some studies

> ### MOVEMENT IS EVERYTHING
>
> My good friend Juli Kagan points out in her wonderful book, *Mind Your Body—Pilates for the Seated Professional*, "The human spine has been sadly neglected. Much of the arthritis and back problems are preventable or at least manageable. Movement is everything. You are as old as your spine is flexible." Using this last criterion, she estimated my age at 92. Just kidding, but I did start Pilates and paying a lot more attention to my posture,

show that we are seven times more likely to be disabled then die during our career.

It is critical to have life insurance to protect your family in case of your death, if you haven't saved enough to take care of them. Don't make the big *mess*take of buying whole or universal life insurance. These pay very high premiums to the insurance agent and are a poor investment vehicle. I suggest buying ten or 20-year level premium term life insurance, which has a low-cost early in our careers when most of us have little money. As we get older, the premiums increase, but so should our assets. Once we reach our early 60s, our children should be off the payroll, and our assets will likely be enough to care for our spouse.

Don't make the big *mess*take of not planning for the care of your family if you should die or be disabled. I know of a prominent dentist who died in a plane crash and left no insurance or assets for his family. His wife had to go back to work for almost minimum wage. This is inexcusable, in my opinion, and tarnished an otherwise outstanding career. Caring for your family is part of finishing well!

Long-term care insurance should also be considered, unless you are very wealthy or very poor. It can cost $100,000 or more annually for nursing home care. This is an emotional decision. I suggest buying one with at least a 90-day waiting period, and one that covers only part of the cost to make the premium payments more reasonable. It will cost you something to live outside a nursing home, so you don't need to insure the entire expense. If you are very poor, the government will often pay for nursing home care.

This is not a complete list of insurances, but the point is that we need to insure against major losses. Insurance is a necessary evil. I don't believe we need to insure against minor losses, so I think we should have a high deductible and self-insure as much as we can afford. It's possible to spend too much money on insurance.

EMBEZZLED!

An often-overlooked way we lose money is through embezzlement. When I worked in my father's restaurant as a child, my dad would allow only family access to the cash register. I thought my dad was just paranoid. Wrong! After being in the dental business for 35 years and hearing many stories of embezzlement, I think this is a legitimate threat to any business.

In my own case, I came within a day of hiring a staff member who had embezzled over $40,000 from her previous dental office. She told me that the previous dentist she worked for was no longer working and couldn't be reached. At the last minute, it occurred to me to go to a dental directory to find this dentist. When I finally reached her, she told me about the embezzlement and obviously advised me not to hire this person.

This near *mess*take reminded me that it is critical to get several references on each employee. It's also important to do background checks before hiring new employees. A case in point is a registered sex offender who was recently accused of molesting a ten-year-old girl at one of our local parks. He was apparently hired by the county to work in the park without the subcontractor doing a background check. Under most state laws, you must get permission from the candidate to perform this background investigation.

Recently an ophthalmology practice in Philadelphia had an office manager who embezzled $780,000 over a four-year period. The office manager did this by submitting false payroll information claiming she was working 20 to 30 hours per day seven days per week! Just remember if you leave money lying around and don't watch it, many people can be subject to the temptation to take it. Don't get lazy in watching your money. I've seen even the most trusted and long-term employees tempted to embezzle. Watch out for an employee who often works late and takes few vacations.

A friend of mine with leukemia underwent bone marrow transplantation in Seattle. While he was gone, his accountant embezzled virtually all of his money thinking that he would never survive. He did. Make it easy for people to be honest by checking everything very closely.

A BAD LEASE

A bad lease with a landlord is another way to lose money. Be very careful what contracts you sign, especially a lease. My son, Dan is a real estate lawyer and says that almost all of these leases are written to be highly favorable to the landlord. In most cases, many of the terms in the lease are negotiable. This is especially so in today's economy. The terms of the lease and your right to renew it should be pre-negotiated when you first sign the lease. These terms need to be very specific because in almost all businesses, your continued occupancy is a critical factor.

A real estate lawyer negotiated my current lease before my son became a real estate lawyer. He negotiated the renewal and the terms of the lease very well. However, we made a big *mess*take by failing to specify that the landlord pay for any costs to fireproof the suite. This cost me about $60,000 for fire protection hidden in the ceiling and the walls. Very painful, so don't forget to include that improvements for fire and disability outside the suite are not your responsibility. Hire a professional to negotiate for you, because even a single word can change the terms and perhaps your life. You don't want to be working most of your life for your banker, the IRS and especially for your landlord.

Another option to consider is to own your own office. This often can work very well especially in smaller towns. In downtown Fort Lauderdale, the cost of property, insurance and taxes make this very expensive. The financial benefits of owning versus leasing should be very carefully evaluated. If you can negotiate a favorable lease then leasing can be more advantageous then owning in some cases.

The Goose that Lays the Golden Egg

Many dentists and other professionals think the grass is greener in other areas. They make investments in restaurants and other businesses and almost always lose a lot of money. I suggest giving up the fantasy of the great investment. I have seen many dentists and others make this big *mess*take. The best way for almost all of us to make money is in our professions where we know what we are doing. This is our most important financial asset!

Probably the most significant way we lose our money is by losing our jobs or our ability to practice our profession. By not doing our job to the best of our ability, or by behaving unethically, we lose our ability to earn money. I know of a local dentist who lost her license because of insurance fraud. Behaving ethically is not only the right thing to do but will also keep us out of financial and legal trouble. In almost all cases, our ability to earn income by working will be our primary asset for much of your life. Almost no investment will return annually what we earn each year.

**Whatever you do, don't kill the goose that lays
the golden egg—your earning potential!**

INVESTMENT PEARLS OF WISDOM

"Plans fail for lack of counsel, but with many advisers they succeed."
Proverbs 15:22

I have gathered the following top ten best pearls of investment wisdom that have stood the test of time and which you can use as a basic guide for your investments.

1. **The classic advice:** My dentist friend who lost his entire pension plan in the Madoff fraud, told me to be sure to reiterate this advice: **If it sounds too good to be true, it is!** If it is so good, why do they need or want your money? Think Madoff and Stanford. It's important to be very vigilant about requests for our money. **Nobody cares as much about your money as you do.**

We learned a lesson about vigilance on a trip down the Amazon River in Peru. On the first night, we went for a hike in the rain forest with my wife, our four boys and a guide. This was described as a fun hike in the jungle with no real danger. We had only been out a few minutes when my wife pointed her flashlight to a tree and asked, "What is that?" The guide responded, "A Fer-de-Lance snake!" This snake is possibly the most poisonous snake in the world. The guide's father had been bitten by one and died. Obviously, we stayed right on the trail and followed the guide closely! It was a great lesson for us to always be attentive, watchful and alert in every aspect of our lives.

Family picture taken the day after our near fatal Amazon jungle hike and, yes, they really do hunt with poison darts! That's a blowgun in his left hand.

2. If something can't go on forever, it won't! How could we believe that tech stocks and houses would continue to appreciate at 20% per year? If you run that out for ten years, stocks and houses would cost eight times more than they did at their high. Who could afford to buy them? The tech-stock dominated NASDAQ index was over 5,000 at its high in March 2000. At the same percentage increase, it would have been at 40,000 in another ten years! This works both ways, however. Now people expect the bad times to go on forever. The NASDAQ index dropped to 1,100 in 2002 and was still at 1,100 in early 2009 but has since recovered to almost 2,200 by November, 2009. Also, don't forget that in 1992 it was at 250 so it is still up considerably over the last 17 years. Houses can't keep going down 3% a month. If they do, eventually they will cost almost nothing to buy.

3. **Time in the market is more important than timing the market.** Market timing is virtually impossible. You have to make two decisions correctly: When to buy and when to sell. There are only two things that you can predict about the stock market. It will fluctuate and eventually it will go up. Eventually, however, sometimes takes a long time.

4. **Return *OF* principal is more important than return *ON* principle.** This makes a lot more sense in 2009 than it did in 1999. Remember, if you lose 50% of your money, as the Dow Jones Industrial Average did in 2008, it takes 100% return on your money to get back your original investment.

It will take over seven years with a 10% return to achieve that.

5. **Save early!** Start saving at least a little, even 1 or 2%, and preferably more, from the very beginning. It develops the habit of saving.

Water the tree before you pick the fruit.

6. **The best source of money is your ability to earn it!** This is the goose that lays your golden eggs.

7. **If you have it made, don't risk it.** Although no investment is risk-free, I was somewhat guilty of this by having 50% of my money still invested in the stock market at age 65. Conversely, if you don't have it made, you will have to take some risk.

8. **Don't confuse genius with a bull market.** This happened between 1982 and 2000 when stocks returned an amazing 18% per year, turning an initial $100,000 into $2 million! Conversely, be gentle with yourself **and don't confuse stupidity with a bear market**, which is what is happening now. From 1998 until mid-2009, the stock market return

has been essentially zero. Recently, I saw a new definition for a bull market—a random market movement causing an investor to mistake himself for a financial genius. And as my mother so wisely said, "Don't take your successes to your head or your failures to your heart."

9. **Think of your dollars saved as freedom fighters.** They are buying you the financial freedom to do and be what you want. After going through some of the best economic times in history since 1980, only a small percentage of people can retire comfortably and most will run out of money before they die.

10. **No matter what, you don't want to be old and poor.** *The Wall Street Journal* reported on February 23, 2009 that many people, even in their 80s, are looking for jobs that pay minimum wage. To avoid this, follow the advice of Solomon, other wise men and these top ten pearls of investment wisdom!

My Personal Investment Philosophy
"An empty stable stays clean, but no income
comes from an empty stable."
Proverbs 14:4

I'm definitely on shaky ground when I start giving investment advice! This is my personal investment philosophy, which would never be confused with Warren Buffett's. It is offered for information purposes only. Please read the financial disclaimer statement at the beginning of the book. As I have said before, I'm not a professional financial planner. I also don't like to spend a lot of my time and energy managing my money. I believe a better use of my time is in earning it and enjoying it. That's why I delegate some of it to a professional "fee only" financial planner. As I've also said before, if you have a winning game, don't change it. If your investments have been doing well, good for you. If not, take a look at some of the principles explained below.

There is no one investment that's right for everyone. Investing depends on the times and on one's temperament. When the financial tide goes out, virtually all the financial boats also go down. Even the most astute investor can lose money when this happens. *Forbes* magazine reports that in 2008 Warren Buffett, arguably the wisest stock market investor of all time, lost $25 billion and Donald Trump lost nearly half of his net worth in real estate. I suggest getting professional advice and then following your own counsel.

Many of my thoughts on investments are covered in the ten pearls listed under financial wisdom, in Solomon's advice to diversify and in the discussion of how not to lose it. In general, I believe the road to financial independence is through my (and Solomon's) first three secrets to financial health: **1. Earn lots. 2. Save lots 3. Don't lose it.** This is the **crucial foundation upon which your financial progress will rest**—regardless of how the economy does and what specific investments you make. Your best investment will almost always be in yourself and enhancing your own income, then saving lots and not losing it. Having said that, no book on financial health would be complete without a discussion about **both** not losing what you have invested and growing your money through investments, so here is mine…

A Fool for a Client

It has been said that the man who is his own lawyer has a fool for a client. I believe the same could be said for the man who does all his own financial planning and investing. It's too complex, and our best efforts are spent on earning money in our own jobs or professions. What I have written is the basics of what you need to know. Hire professionals, including lawyers, accountants and fee-only certified financial planners, to help you with the details and implementation. You need to be knowledgeable, but it's extremely difficult to know as much as the professionals.

If possible, hire a fee-only certified financial planner to advise you. While financial planners often charge 1 to 2% of the assets they manage, their incentive to increase your wealth is that increasing your assets, in turn, increases their income. What they do best is get you organized and prevent you from making the poor investments and big *mess*takes from which it is very difficult to recover. They can also help you immensely with retirement planning, and how to manage your assets and withdrawal rate in retirement. Few people have the talent and want to use their time and energy to manage their own finances. If this is your passion and you are good at it, then go for it. However, these people who completely manage their own investments generally don't meet with their spouse/significant other or other advisers on a regular basis to go over their finances. The value of having a financial planner is that these meetings will occur regularly and will help you keep your focus on controlling spending, savings goals and investment goals.

Ron Blue, the founder of one of the largest financial planning firms in the country and the author of the bestseller, *Master Your Money*, describes financial planning simply as "allocating limited financial resources among unlimited alternatives." By this criterion, even the richest man in the world, Bill Gates, would need financial planning. Ron Blue adds that the biggest financial *mess*take we make is "a consumptive lifestyle."

Of course, the responsibility for managing your money ultimately rests with you and your spouse or life partner. Nobody cares for your money as much as you do. Ignorance is definitely not bliss when it comes to money. You need to learn what you can about money. This book and the books in the bibliography will help you. As my father said, "To train a dog, you need to be smarter than the dog." We need to be knowledgeable in all areas of our life, maybe not smarter than some of our advisors, but at least well informed.

My dad lived through the Depression. There was no FDIC insurance at the time and fear of bank failures was widespread. As a result, he buried some of his money in the backyard and also put some under the mattress to protect it from loss.

While I recommend a conservative investment style, I definitely don't recommend burying it or putting your money under the mattress as my dad did. When my dad finally dug up the money, water seepage had destroyed some of it. In addition, money will make the mattress very difficult to sleep on and the return on the investment will be very low.

The classic 1949 investment guide *The Intelligent Investor* has been praised by Warren Buffett as "by far the best book on investing ever written." Its author, Benjamin Graham was one of the first to recommend a more conservative asset allocation between stocks and bonds. He advised splitting your money equally between stocks and bonds. Graham added that your stock proportion should never go below 25% (when you think stocks are expensive and bonds are cheap) or above 75% (when stocks seem cheap).

John Bogle, the founder of the Vanguard Mutual Fund Group, modified this by suggesting that you invest your age in bonds. This simple formula will not work for everyone, however, depending on your circumstances and how much money you have, it's a good place to start. For example, if you are 40 years old, you would have 40% of your money in well diversified bond type investments and 60% of your money in well diversified stock type funds. At age 67, my current age, you would have 67% of your money in bonds. New era advice suggests subtracting your age from 120 and using that number to determine the percent you would allocate to stock investments. For some investors, the big concern here was that they were missing out on the increase in stocks, which would offset inflation. What was missing, however, was the risk of loss with deflation. I would rather leave some money on the table, even if stocks do go up, and pay a little, or even a lot more, for basic services than risk losing my money and not being able to pay for any services. The long-term difference between the returns on stocks and bonds is not as great as commonly projected, with considerable more risk for stocks. In fact, as of June 30, 2009, long-term treasury bonds have outperformed stocks over the past 25 years, according to Jason Zweig in *The Wall Street Journal.* The basic rule is: if you have it made (i.e., enough money saved for retirement), don't risk it. Another basic rule: hope for the best, but plan for the worst. No investment is risk free; however, bonds are generally less risky than stocks, depending on what type of bond you buy, of course.

With the amount of money the government is printing, I do expect inflation to return eventually, but in retirement, inflation is not as big a threat as some warn you it is. Once you're retired for a while, the things on which you spend your money, such as food and gasoline, may inflate, but these are not really large expenses. If you spend $500 a month on food and it quadruples to $2,000 per month, this is still not a relatively large expense. If you have your home and car paid off, and have no debt, then inflation in these areas will only be a minor inconvenience. If you're living only on Social Security, then these increases in food, transportation and healthcare can be major. Hopefully, if you follow the advice in this book, that won't be the case, so don't lose sleep over inflation if you've saved a reasonable amount and have no debt.

Young people with many years to work before retirement still have to be somewhat concerned about inflation. However, even they should stay with the tried and true, which is to invest your age in bonds. For example, at age 30, have 30% of your money in bonds. You can modify that by five to 10% either way, depending on the price earnings multiples of the stock market. If the price earning multiple is far above the long-term average

> ### CONSUMER PRICE INDEX
>
> The government calculates the consumer price index using 43% for housing costs; 16% for food; 15% for transportation; 6% each for healthcare and recreation; 4% each for clothing and education; and 3% each for communication and other. If you have your home and car paid off, don't pay anything for education and little for clothing, then over 50% of the inflation index doesn't affect you. The government has considered establishing a consumer price index for the elderly, although the new proposed index doesn't change things much. One thing that does go up in retirement is health care costs. These need to be planned for with savings, insurance and long-term care insurance, if appropriate.

of about 16 times earnings, then put less in stocks. If the price to earnings ratio is well below 16, then put more money in stocks and less in bonds. Historically, stocks are overpriced when they are well above 16 times earnings, and underpriced when they are well below 16 times earnings.

I suggest using the "normalized" price to earnings ratio (P/E ratio) created by Yale University professor Robert Shiller. Shiller smoothes out the data over 10 years to remove short-term volatility. For example, with earnings very low now, the P/E earnings ratio in the fall of 2009 for the Standard and Poor 500 stock index is over 100–in record territory. The normalized ratio at that time was about 18. This ratio adjusts for unusual trends caused by using trailing earnings or projected earnings as a basis for investing.

The challenge is finding the "normalized" price to earnings ratio. I have listed in the appendix how to find this "normalized" ratio.

This ratio is the ratio of the price of the stock to the earnings of the stock. For example, if the price of the stock is $16 and the earnings per share are $1, then the price to earnings ratio is 16/1. Knowing this ratio at least lets us know whether stocks are cheap or expensive by historical standards. Hopefully, we can then keep our heads about us when prices get really high, as they did in 2000, just before the crash, when they reached nearly 45 times earnings or lower when they reached eight times earnings as they did in 1980. This was just before the longest bull market in history. During 2008, the P/E ratio took on an additional meaning: the percentage of investors wetting their pants as the market kept crashing.

DIVERSIFICATION

Because of the failure of asset allocation strategies in 2008, the current market uncertainty and the threat of inflation and rising interest rates, it's a good idea to add extra diversification to your portfolio. Unless we have many different asset classes, we may not be as well diversified as we think. During the last market crash in 2008, conventional asset allocation did not work because those that diversified into large and small cap US stocks, and international and emerging market stocks, saw them all go down at the same time. The asset classes were too narrow and too highly correlated.

One current recommendation is to have alternative investments that don't correlate so as to have some asset classes up when the others are down. It does make sense to include riskier alternative investments, such as real estate through REIT's, gold funds, international and emerging market funds, commodity funds, energy funds, and even some hedge funds, as small parts of our long-term asset allocation. With the world's population due to rise two billion people to 8.5 billion people in the next 20 years, it seems likely that commodities and energy will become more valuable. These would all be part of your portfolio that's allocated to stocks. Because of the risk of losing all of your money in hedge funds, I would limit them to no more than 5% of my stock portfolio. This more involved asset allocation can get complicated and is why I suggest using a certified financial planner.

Your bond portfolio can also be diversified into corporate bonds, high yield bonds, treasuries, municipal bonds, foreign debt, cash and treasury inflation protected securities. And once again, Solomon nailed it 3,000 years ago when he recommended diversifying into seven or eight asset classes.

Matthew Tuttle emphasizes this broader asset allocation model in his book, *How Harvard and Yale Beat the Market*. This investment model will likely reduce the chances of large losses like those most people experienced in 2000 and 2008, but it should be remembered it will also reduce gains in an up market. That's okay with me, but it might concern less risk-averse investors.

And Tuttle's book is another example of the difficulties of designing a system to beat the market. It was published just before Harvard lost about 30% of its portfolio for the 2009 fiscal year because of a much larger allocation in hedge funds and illiquid investments which I don't recommend.

"If the scheme was so great," Tuttle says in his book, "why would someone sell the scheme rather than trade it for themselves?" Yet he then goes on to promote the Harvard and Yale system. In fact, as soon as someone publishes a book on a new terrific scheme for beating the market, it usually means the system will soon no longer work for us unsuspecting amateur investors.

If you are concerned about inflation, one investment to consider is Treasury Inflation-Protected Securities. These investments are adjusted to increase the return to match inflation. As an additional means of diversification, I put a small amount of my money in these securities. This is an investment primarily used for insurance against the possibility of inflation. In fact, TIPS and gold have been practically the only negatively correlated assets since 1973. Since you have to pay taxes each year on the income, these are often best placed in a tax-deferred retirement plan. Vanguard has an excellent low-cost fund for these plans. This would be part of my bond allocation of about 67%, which again, matches my age.

So there you have it; a foolproof, fail-safe, risk-free strategy for financial peace of mind!

Just kidding. It does not exist. I suggest we give up searching for this Holy Grail for investing. As Solomon says, earn lots, save lots, diversify to minimize losses, and then enjoy it. Just keep reading, the simple secrets to financial peace of mind will be revealed in Chapter Six!

Bubbles and Manias

In what almost qualifies as ancient wisdom, Charles Mackay writes about our inability to think rationally about investments in his famous 1841 book, *Extraordinary Popular Delusions and the Madness of Crowds*. Mackay discusses the Dutch Tulip financial mania of the early 17th century, in which some tulip bulbs were bid up to as much as 400 pounds sterling each. It is a mania strikingly similar to the recent Internet stock bubble of 2000 and the real estate bubble of 2006. He wrote: "Men, it has been well said, think in herds; it will be seen that they go mad in herds, while they only recover their senses slowly, and one by one."

About the South Sea Company trade monopoly bubble in the early 18th century, Mackay wrote, "Men were no longer satisfied with the slow but sure profits of cautious industry. The hope of boundless wealth for the morrow made them heedless and extravagant for today." Does this remind you of our recent manias including 1929?

> *"Some of the people I know lost millions, I was luckier. All I lost was $240,000. I would've lost more, but that was all the money I had."*
> Groucho Marx, 1929

Many of us including Groucho could have saved a lot of money and probably would be able to sleep better if we had read Mackay's book before these manias. Groucho claimed that the financial trauma of losing his entire savings in 48 hours gave him insomnia for the rest of his life.

We need to be ever mindful of the madness of the "fear and greed herds." We saw a fear bubble recently when treasury bills were paying slightly less than 0% for one day. People were so fearful they actually gave their money to the government and accepted slightly less back just to preserve their capital. What is the next bubble? Keep an eye out—it will come.

The next bubble to burst might be in commercial real estate. According to a recent article in *The Wall Street Journal*, "There are more commercial-mortgage-backed securities outstanding than credit card debt, student loans and car loans combined and many of these loans are going bad rapidly." Most of this debt is scheduled to come due in 2011 and 2012. It should be interesting.

It's good to keep an eye on what Yale professor Robert Shiller says. He correctly called the 2000 bubble in stocks and the 2007 bubble in housing. In his book, *Irrational Exuberance*, he writes, "Irrational exuberance is the psychological basis for all speculative bubbles." In every speculative bubble there is always widespread consensus that "this time it's different." This consensus is used to justify each market's irrational exuberance.

It seems like we should just follow Professor Shiller's advice on investing. However February 25, 2009, he said he would not buy stocks now because he thinks they will go even lower. This was just before one of the greatest bull markets in history from March 9 through November 2009 when the stock market went up over 60% in eight months. He might yet be right, time will tell.

Superstar investor Jim Rogers has this advice for his daughters in his book *A Gift to My Children, A Father's Lessons for Life and Investing:* "What is happening now has happened before and will happen again. Be extremely doubtful when you have people proclaiming, 'It's different this time.' Historically, nothing emerges as so entirely different; such claims are indicative of mass hysteria."

To determine when we are in the next mania or bubble, you can use some of the criteria outlined by John Kenneth Galbraith in his book, *A Short History of Financial Euphoria*, as "increased leverage, conspicuous consumption and at the end, amateurs enter the market."

It's good to be reminded to keep our heads about us as Rudyard Kipling does in his famous poem "If," partly excerpted below:

If you can keep your head about you when all about you

Are losing theirs and blaming it on you.

If you can trust yourself when all men doubt you,

But make allowance for their doubting too;

Yours is the Earth and everything that's in it,

And, which is more—you'll be a Man—my son!

AMATEURS ENTER THE MARKET!

Sensing that too many amateurs were in the market, Joseph Kennedy, the father of President John Kennedy, sold most of his stocks just before the stock market crash in 1929 when he got a stock tip from his shoe shine boy. During the technology stock boom in 2000, my hygienist kept CNBC on the television in her room and bragged about how much money she and her friends were making in the stock market. In addition, my wife called me when I was visiting my ill father in Illinois and said, "We need to buy some tech stocks." One of her tennis playing partners was also bragging about how much money she was making. The final straw was when my dental study group had a meeting in Denver to discuss with a prominent stock analyst from Janus Investments how to invest in technology stocks. That's when I knew that the end was near! It started down three days later. Fortunately, investing in tech stocks is one **mess**take I did not make.

Watch investment costs carefully. Management fees, transaction costs and taxes can easily take away 2 to 3% or more of your returns. Jason Zweig tells a story in *The Wall Street Journal* on August 15, 2009 that he heard from a former mutual fund industry chief executive, "I sat in on a management meeting where senior guy said, 'This funds performance is so bad, all the investors must either be dead or dumb. Nobody will object if we raise the fees.' It became: 'Let's raise the fees, just because we can.'"

One way to pay more attention to fees is to figure the expense in dollars in addition to percentages. For example, if you have $500,000 invested and the fee is 1.5%, then the dollar cost is $7,500. Then decide if you're getting good value for the management fee. If you have $5 million invested and the total fees are 2%, then you are paying $100,000 per year to have your money managed. This helps us see more clearly what we are paying and decide if we're getting good value.

Be sure that you look at your real returns after expenses. As I mentioned in Chapter 3, I am a fan of the very low-cost Vanguard index funds, created by John Bogle, for a portion of one's investments. Many of these funds charge a custodial fee of only .22% or less, which is almost 1% less than many other managed funds. Their Life Strategy funds are made up of index funds with asset allocations ranging from 20 to 90% stocks. This gives you several options, depending on your age and risk tolerance.

Recently, these funds also have been down, especially if they had a high stock allocation. I suggest you follow John Bogle's recommendation of allocating your age to bonds, which would have put 67% in bonds in my case, and would have significantly mitigated any losses. My own losses at the bottom were about 30%. If I had followed Bogle's allocation, they probably would've been closer to 15%. I still had enough after my loss, but it certainly got my attention and made me glad that I had not quit my job.

INDIVIDUAL STOCKS AND BROKERS

I'm not a big fan of buying individual stocks. I tried doing this for awhile when I was younger and for me it was a big *mess*take. I lost money almost every time.

In the best of years, only a minority of the managed mutual funds beat the averages. This is also true for managed bond funds. The June 1, 2009 issue of *The Wall Street Journal* reports that since 1999, there's been only one year that the average bond fund topped the index.

I don't recommend individual stocks because you have to make two decisions correctly on when to buy and when to sell. In addition, I believe your time is best used maximizing your earnings in your own job or profession. If you use a stockbroker frequently, you'll likely end up "broker." They make money only through commissions made trading. One of their jobs is to sell you the product their company is currently pushing, which often has a higher commission than other products. The analysts for these brokerage firms are often simply touts for the stocks they are promoting, and seldom have the courage to issue sell recommendations. They should be ignored completely. They have too much conflict of interest. Supposedly, this situation has improved since they were sued after the 2000 crash.

BROKERS?

As I prepared to write this book, I encountered several stories from former brokers that were disturbing. One of the most disturbing is told by former stock broker Matthew Tuttle in his book, *How Harvard and Yale Beat the Market*. "When I started, one of the grizzled veterans came over to talk to me. He told me to cold call like crazy and once I got a client to make lots of trades. He said I would probably blow up [lose most or all of my client's money] half my clients. Half would leave and half would stay until I blew them up again. But by continuing to add new clients, I was guaranteed a six-figure salary." Obviously, this doesn't apply to all brokers. Just be very careful and look at your results over time if you do use one.

In the same vein, famous investor Bernard Baruch said, "Never pay the slightest attention to what a company president says about his stock." Obviously, company presidents have the same conflict of interest as their analysts.

"Only simpletons believe everything they are told!
The prudent carefully consider their steps."
Proverbs 14:15

Earlier, I talked about getting conflicting advice. Many investment advisors are now saying that the buy-and-hold investment index fund philosophy is dead. I heard a prominent professional money advisor say recently that, with the projected future low returns of the stock market, the best plan is to buy individual stocks low and then sell them high, implying that he and his managers could do this. Actually this is just the opposite of what most

> **THE DARTS WIN!**
>
> Consider the 17-year Wall Street Journal contest in which the staff throws darts at a list of stocks and experienced readers carefully choose their best stock. Six stocks in each group are followed for six months. As of November 2009, the darts have won the contest 21 times beating the 14 wins for the readers' best stock selections. This is a 60% winning percentage for the darts!

people do. Most were buying stocks in early 2008 when they were very high and then sold them later in early 2009 after they had dropped dramatically. They bought high and sold low based on emotions missing a huge rally in 2009.

John Bogle notes, "It's a fool's game, if you want to trade the market, you've got to be right twice—you've got to get out and get back in at the right time." Almost nobody has been able to do this consistently over time. Possibly the most successful stock picker over the two decades was Bill Miller. His Legg Mason Value fund once beat the market 15 years in a row! This fund lost a mind-boggling 55% in 2008 and has been one of the worst funds in its category for the last three years.

In *Money* magazine's June 2009 issue, William Bernstein, the author of *The Four Pillars of Investing* wrote, "Remember that the point of investing isn't to aim for the highest possible returns. It's to make sure you don't die poor. Yet trying to optimize your performance by seeking out the needles in the haystack (picking the top performing stocks) is a sure way of becoming, well, poor."

Municipal Bonds and Future Government Liabilities

I also believe in keeping a portion of one's investments in high-grade municipal bonds. I'm particularly thankful I did this during the last decade of the stock market's performance. Purchase only the highest-grade AA or AAA general obligation municipal bonds (those backed by unlimited power to tax) and buy individual bonds that you can hold until maturity. By doing this, you avoid the ups and downs in their value caused by changes in interest rates. For example, if interest rates go up, the value of the bonds, if sold that day, go down and vice versa. If you hold the municipal bond until maturity, this does not affect you.

As we are seeing in California, the state government doesn't have enough revenue to operate. This California-style time bomb is about to explode as spending remains the same, but tax revenues collapse. There's a huge problem growing in pension benefits for government employees (teachers, firemen, policemen, etc.) who retire on two-thirds or more of their final gross salary after just 20 years. Some even retire at 100% of their salary after 30 years. Many of these pensions are based on the average earnings of the employees' top three or five years, which they often inflate by working lots of overtime in their final years. This is called pension spiking and is very common. The costs of this increased pension last for the lifetime of the retirees who often retire in their mid-40s or early 50s. Most have full medical benefits, and many have inflation adjustments. Some even go back to work the next day after retiring. Baby boomers will start turning 65 in 2011 and by 2030, 20% of the US population will be 65 or older. This means that pension and Social Security payouts will be rising rapidly over the next 20 years.

> ### GOVERNMENT BENEFITS
>
> If you think I'm exaggerating about government employee benefits, read what Michael Mayo wrote in the *South Florida Sun Sentinel* in June 2009, about a recent contract signed by the local sheriff's department, "There are enough sweeteners to kill a diabetic." After 11 years, deputies get 45 paid days off annually— 21 vacation days, 12 sick days, 11 holidays and one personal day. Unused sick days and comp time can be carried over for decades and cashed out upon retirement—up to 28 weeks—and it's paid at the final salary rate, not when it was earned.

Who wouldn't like to have these pension plans and these benefits? No private company could possibly afford it. Soon no government agency will be able to afford it either and some will likely go bankrupt, as some cities like Vallejo, California already have. In the June 11, 2009, *The Wall Street Journal*, Arthur Laffer reports the unfunded liabilities of federal programs, such as Social Security, civil service and military pensions, Medicare and Medicaid, are over the $100 trillion mark. Total federal tax receipts are $2.4 trillion, which means that liabilities are over 40 times one year's income. If we add the $1.5 trillion cost projected over the next 10 years for a government-run medical plan, the numbers become even more problematic. And the cost will likely be much more, based on many previous government under-projections.

As baby boomers retire, the Government Accountability Office estimates that, if current government policies continue, by 2040, interest on our national debt will absorb 30% of all tax revenues, and entitlements like Social Security, government pensions and Medicare will absorb the rest, leaving nothing for defense or education or anything else. These enormous liabilities seem to me like the *huge iceberg the Titanic* approached at full speed, despite

Future government liabilities

being warned. We know how that ended. For younger people, this huge debt will have a big impact on their financial lives in the form of higher taxes and fewer government benefits.

Can the basic rules of financial health be so grossly ignored forever by our governments? No individual business entity or person could survive these shortfalls. This enormous pension liability is a major reason for the failure of many companies, such as General Motors, which guaranteed full retirement after 30 years with a supplement to match Social Security up to age 62. If you went to work for GM at age 18, you could retire with full benefits at age 48, with a Social Security supplement, until Social Security began paying at age 62.

YOUR RISK TOLERANCE?

For my wife and I and our temperaments, it's important to be able to sleep well with our investments, so we don't make risky investments. We have a low risk tolerance. If your risk tolerance is higher, you may prefer riskier investments. That's fine. Just be sure you can truly tolerate the greater chance of loss that comes with the greater chance of gain. During the last few years, some people discovered they weren't as tolerant of risk as they thought. I have enough things to disturb my sleep without having a lot of risky investments out there. In the past, conventional wisdom was the more risk, the more reward. Vanguard founder John Bogle points out that, "The stock market isn't a place for betting. The place for betting is called Las Vegas." Recently, we've learned the more risk, the more risk of loss!

Warren Buffett, who said, "When forced to choose, I will not trade even a night's sleep for the chance of extra profits," shares this view. Bernard Baruch, another of this country's great investors, said to a friend who lay awake at night worrying about his investments, "Sell down to the sleeping point." Having said that, don't make any rash decisions based on one or two nights lost sleep. Listen to the ancient wisdom of Greek playwright Euripides in 425 BC, "Second thoughts are ever wiser." Check with your financial advisors before making any quick decisions.

A joke about investing defines the institutional investor—a past year investor who is now locked up in a psychiatric ward. Unless you want to make yourself crazy, I don't believe it's a good idea to watch the stock market daily or real estate prices monthly. It is a good idea to recheck one's investments every three to six months to see how things are going and make minor adjustments. We're interested in how the investments look in five, ten, 20 or more years, depending on when and for what we need the money. Warren Buffett points out that if you plant trees, you don't worry about the growth each year. Some years will be better than others. You know that in 20 years it's very likely you'll have a nice sized tree. He recommends the same philosophy for money investments. It's worked pretty well for him!

The Tortoise and the Hare

This philosophy is illustrated well in Aesop's fable, "The Tortoise and the Hare." As we will remember, the hare got far ahead of the tortoise early in the race and decided to rest after his big gains. The tortoise just put one foot in front of the other and with small steps won the race.

Slow and steady also wins the race in investments

RETIREMENT—THE $ NUMBER

One of the primary objectives of financial health is a financially secure retirement. We achieve this primarily by being financially independent. The question sometimes consumes us: How much money will I need? There are many complex formulas available. The simplest is to multiply your pre-tax retirement income by 20. For example, if you need $75,000 in retirement income per year, you will need $1.5 million in savings. If you spend $150,000 a year, then you will need almost three million in savings. This would allow you to withdraw 5.3% of your money each year for 30 years with only a 1% chance of running out of money at the end of 30 years. This formula is based on the so-called "Monte Carlo" simulation that examines thousands of possible market scenarios. Ben Stein and Phil DeMuth brilliantly calculate this in their book, *Yes, You Can Still Retire Comfortably!*

One way to reduce the number needed for retirement is simply to reduce expenses. Instead of spending $150,000 per year, spend $100,000 or $50,000. This reduces your number needed for retirement from $3 million to $2 million and to $1 million if you reduce your expenses to $50,000 per year. I'll show you how to predictably accumulate this $1 million and even more in the next section.

Another way to reduce this number is to work a few years longer if you can. I discussed the benefits of this earlier in the book under "Don't Quit Your Job Too Early." If you work five years longer, this reduces the number needed by approximately 10% since you will be using the money for five years less. It also gives you five more years to accumulate and reach your number. In fact, it seems that for those where this is possible, "The Magill Report" states that, "Age 70 is rapidly becoming the new 65 as the target date for retirement."

Remember that, in retirement, for the first few years your expenses may be similar to your pre-retirement expenses. However, later on, most expenses will diminish significantly. When my father was in his 80s, he seemed to live on air with very low expenditures. When you add in Social Security income, many times by the time you reach your mid-70s, you will only need 50 to 75% of your pre-retirement income to live comfortably. If you use 100% of your income for your retirement projections, the numbers get huge and discouraging.

One caveat, if you lose a lot of money in the first few years, then the 5.3% withdrawal amount will likely not work out. In this simulation, if you take out only 3.5% of your money, it's 100% safe in any scenario. If at all possible, pay off your mortgage and all major debt before you retire. It's important to reevaluate our investment returns and personal expenses every few years to see if we need to reduce our expenses and withdrawal rate. We need to be certain that we don't run out of money before we run out of life, which would be a very bad ending.

How to Predictably Retire a Millionaire

It's not that hard if you follow what is called "The No Hope Investment Plan" by Kendrick Mercer and Albert Goerig (who happens to be a dentist) in their terrific book, *Time and Money*. This plan means you do not live in the hope that the stock market or real estate goes up 10 to 15% annually so that you'll

have enough money for retirement and other needs. It means you won't have to hope and take risks, if you saved lots and diversified it carefully in conservative investments, even if you realized only a 6% return.

Here's how the "No Hope Investment Plan" to achieve financial independence works. Someone with a $48,000 annual income who starts saving at age 35, $12,000 a year or $230 per week in tax-deferred savings, and earns only 6%, at age 65 will have $1,005,620. That person will be a millionaire! That person could withdraw 5.3% or $53,000 per year for 30 years with only a 1% chance he or she would run out of money. In addition, that person would have Social Security income. An 8% return would result in $1,468,180. I suggest going with the more conservative 6% return because future stock market returns may be lower, and I suggest part of the portfolio be put in bonds.

Because of possible lower future returns, it will also likely be necessary to save more, hence the 25% savings rate suggested above. The U.S. Census Bureau estimates the median family income for a family of four in 2009 at $70,354, so they could possibly save more than $12,000 per year. Using the illustration above, this is why I say almost anyone can predictably retire a millionaire if they start saving early.

A person with $120,000 income and $40,000 in tax deferred savings each year, a 33% savings rate, would have $3,352,067 at age 65. This person could then withdraw $165,000 per year until age 95 before running out of money. The way you save this much money is to put it in your retirement plans before tax. There will be tax when the money is withdrawn. This is purposely a conservative plan because having enough is more important, in my mind, than having more. If you've reached enough, there is no need to be gambling for more when you could lose much or all of it.

I know this 6% return sounds boring and won't play well at cocktail parties, but let's look at it again using the rule of 72. If you divide six into 72, your money will double in 12 years. Although that doesn't sound that great, let's look at some alternatives. Suppose you have invested in a hedge fund that returned 15% each year for the past six years. Now you really have something to brag about at cocktail parties. You even did better than Madoff! But let's look closer at this. After fees and multiple charges, which usually run about 20% of the profit and 2% of the amount invested, your return was probably only 12%. That's still great and your money will double in only six years.

But here's the rest of the story. What if in year seven you lost 25% of your money? This is not uncommon. A case in point is Harvard, which lost 30% of its endowment fund for the fiscal year ending June 2009. And their investments are managed by the supposedly best and brightest. Now let's look at the same $100,000 invested in boring AA rated corporate bonds, or taxable municipal bonds, paying 6% a year. Assuming both investments are in taxdeferred retirement plans, at the end of seven years, which investment will end up with the most money?

With the hedge fund, if you started out with $100,000 invested, after six years you will have $200,000, but after seven years and your 25% loss, you will only have $150,000. With the boring 6% return, after seven years you will have $158,000, $8,000 more, and earned with minimal risk. The tortoise beats the hare again!

Don't Retire—Rediscover Your Purpose

When we visited Masai villages in Kenya we brought along soccer balls and pencils for their schools. I also brought along dental instruments for the dental school in Nairobi and gave a lecture to the faculty on simple, economical treatments for periodontal disease. The Masai are very happy people even though they live in houses made out of cow dung with no air conditioning. I still can't get Brenda to try this.

As Dr. Nancy Schlossberg writes in her excellent book, *Retire Smart, Retire Happy*, "Most of us eagerly look forward to our retirement from full-time work, but the reality of retirement can be very different." She adds, "Retirement is *scary*. And why shouldn't it be? So many aspects of our life are suddenly in flux."

I don't recommend retirement, especially as if it is defined by withdrawal. This is what we are trying to avoid in our lives. This is good news for most people since they won't have enough money to retire comfortably anyway. I recommend continuing to grow and develop. If you have saved enough, think of this not as a time to earn more money, but a time for renewal and rediscovery. Don't retire from life when you retire from full-time paid employment. Lloyd Reeb discusses this attitude in detail in his book, *From Success to Significance: When the Pursuit of Success Isn't Enough*. He speaks about the importance of staying vital and how to realign your priorities and then actively put these new priorities into practice.

Let's not overlook the many benefits that we derive from what is commonly called work. My work allows me to continue to feel good about myself by making a contribution to my patients and my coworkers. It's good for my self-esteem and adds variety to my life. My relationships with my partner, teammates, patients and colleagues add tremendously to the quality of my life. It's also good for my relationship with my wife for us to have some time apart. There's more

> ### Just Get Over It!
> In a June 21, 2009 *Wall Street Journal* article, "Why Your Cubicle Moonlights as a Therapist," psychotherapist Peter Kramer of Brown University points out, "The office teaches all of us when to stand our ground and when to be strategic. The workplace says, 'Aw, get over yourself.' Since on the job we're focused on performance, we're likely to do just that, to absorb advice and move on."

than a grain of truth in the jokes, "For better or for worse, but not for lunch," and "Retirement means half as much money and twice as much spouse."

Even if you have to stay working for financial reasons, don't forget the many benefits you get from your work. Continuing to work part-time as I have been able to do provides possibly the best of both worlds.

GIVING IS RECEIVING

As I cut back my work schedule, it allowed me to make a bigger contribution in other areas. For example, I lecture on practice and life management to the senior dental students at the local dental school. This is something they desperately need and is a passion of mine. It brings me joy and also allowed me time to write this book and lecture to other groups. I hope this will make a contribution to the world by helping people with their struggles with money and life. We're all in this together, so by sharing my struggles with life and money, I learn and grow myself. By helping others, I help myself, an important life lesson for all of us.

Scott Peck in his book, *The Road Less Traveled,* points out that personal development and growth is never over. If possible, continue to work at least part-time at something you have a passion for. This has been proven to delay both physical and cognitive decline.

WHY YOU SHOULD DELAY TAKING SOCIAL SECURITY

Another part of retirement income is Social Security. For high-income people, this may not be completely available when they retire and will likely be taxed. The government will need some way to fund its operations by reducing or taxing some of these benefits. In 2009, the government is borrowing 45% of its budget. For most people, Social Security will continue to be available. It would be political suicide to eliminate it or even reduce it by much.

This benefit should not be minimized since $25,000 of Social Security income is equivalent to a municipal bond portfolio of $500,000 earning 5% tax-free. It's also inflation-adjusted which the municipal bond portfolio would not be. It's not unusual for professionals to max out with $28,000 per year in benefits at age

66 with spouses receiving at least $14,000 in spousal benefits. This would be even more at age 70. It's good to remember that this is our money that we paid into a fund. The government has spent it to fund current operations and now will have trouble paying it back. Like many people, the government spent their retirement funds. It's also good to remember that this was never meant to be our only income in retirement. Don't make the big *mess*take of using this as your only retirement income. It won't be enough for most people.

I suggest waiting until age 70 to take Social Security benefits rather than taking the benefits at the earliest age available, which is 62. The final benefit increases 8% for each year we wait, which means we will get 64% more money at age 70. My estimated benefit at age 70 would be $3,201 per month. This is significant. Three-fourths start the benefit at age 62. This is not surprising in an era characterized by poor long-term financial planning. Again, we don't want to be poor at the end of our life. I would rather have the security of having a larger paycheck at 85 than regretting that I left some money on the table if I die at age 75.

Another important issue is that the higher earning spouse will allow his or her surviving spouse to receive his full benefit if he waits until age 70 to start drawing benefits. If the higher earning spouse takes the benefit early, his or her surviving spouse's benefits will be permanently reduced. Again, part of finishing well is making sure that your spouse will be well taken care of. A spouse who waits until age 70 to take the benefits will substantially increase the benefits to his or her survivor over the long-term. Investigate all this closely before you take the Social Security benefit at age 62. Go to socialsecurity.gov for more information. You can even specifically calculate your own retirement benefit as I did.

As I keep saying, reasonable and responsible people can differ on most of the ideas that I have presented in this chapter. Investigate and decide for yourself.

What ideas for not losing your money do you want to implement and/or pass on as your legacy to others?

_____

_____

_____

_____

_____

_____

_____

_____

_____

_____

_____

_____

CHAPTER FIVE

The Fourth Secret: "Enjoy!"

"It's good for one to eat and to drink and to
enjoy the fruits of all his labor."
Ecclesiastes 5:18

I came across the following quote while visiting Egypt. It is from an Egyptian pharaoh who lived 500 years before Solomon. Again, the ancients really did know it long ago.

"More pleasurable is the bread when the heart
is happy than richness with sorrow."
Amenophis 1570 BC

Understanding Money and Happiness

Money is something we choose to trade our life energy for and can be a terrific servant or a tyrannical master.

"Happy is the person who finds
wisdom and gains understanding.
For the profit of wisdom is
better than silver, and her
wages are better than gold."
Proverbs 3:13

There is considerable evidence that money, at least beyond a certain amount, doesn't buy much additional happiness. The Harvard psychology professor, Daniel Gilbert, talks about this in his book, *Stumbling on Happiness*. He points out that, "It hurts to be hungry, cold and scared, but once you have bought your way out of these burdens, the rest of your money is an increasingly useless pile of paper."

Jason Zweig, in his intriguing book, *Your Money and Your Brain*, says that one of the great discoveries of neuroeconomics is that expectation is more intense than experience. The thought of getting rich or hitting the jackpot is more pleasant for many people than the reality of getting rich or hitting the jackpot. This is the central reason why so many people were unhappy, even when they had unbelievable affluence, before the recession. Unfortunately, many of us don't learn from our *mess*take

WINNING THE LOTTERY AND HAPPINESS

Brickman, Coates, and Janoff-Bulman published a groundbreaking study in the *Journal of Personality and Social Psychology* in 1978.

Lottery winners and individuals who sustained a serious physical injury were both studied to determine if winning the lottery made them happier and if sustaining an injury made them less happy. What the study found was that immediately after either event, levels of happiness were higher for lottery winners and lower for those physically injured, but that after eight weeks or less, both groups of people returned to the level of happiness they had before the event.

This research suggests that we adapt to both positive and negative events very quickly, and often return to the degree of happiness we had before the event.

Because we adapt constantly, Brickman coined the term "hedonic treadmill," that is, we have to constantly seek out higher levels of reward just to maintain the same level of subjective pleasure.

We need to be sure we haven't lost the things that money has a limited ability to buy: relationships, health, happiness and meaning.

and think that if we only had more money or more material things again, we will be happy.

Since 1950, studies show our standard of living has almost tripled. Yet there is no change in our level of happiness. The same is true in China and Japan, even after huge increases in the standard of living over the past 30 years. How can this be explained?

It turns out that we tend to adapt in a short time to almost all changes in quality of life and increased income. Our happiness tends to be based on our closest social comparisons. When others' relative incomes go up similarly to ours, there is no net change in our happiness level. If everybody's income goes up, we don't realize much change in our level of happiness; and if our income goes up a lot, we soon adapt to our new riches and our spending usually rises to the level of our new income. This adaptation to new riches has an intriguing flipside. We will also adapt to changes on the downside, as has happened to most of us recently. We will gradually adapt to losing money and our misery will dissipate substantially.

FIVE WAYS MONEY CAN CONTRIBUTE TO OUR HAPPINESS:

1. Earn a higher income than most of those to whom you compare yourself.

2. Or, save more than most of those to whom you compare yourself.

Charles Dickens dispenses this advice on money and happiness in his mostly autobiographical book, *David Copperfield*. His character, Mr. Micawber, who ends up in debtor's prison bemoans, "Annual income twenty pounds, annual expenditure nineteen, nineteen six, result: happiness.

Annual income twenty pounds, annual expenditure twenty pounds ought and six, result: misery."

Dickens knew well what he was talking about. His father was sent to debtors' prison when Charles was 12 years old, forcing Charles to work long hours in miserable conditions to help pay off the family debt. His personal experience as a child laborer inspired some of his other books, including Oliver Twist.

Can you imagine if we had a debtor's prison now? Would you be in or out?

3. Change your comparisons to those in poorer countries, such as India or Africa, and to less fortunate colleagues.

4. To fight adaptation to more money, remind yourself constantly to be grateful for your good fortune and to savor it.

5. And finally…enjoy it wisely!

"Every increased possession loads us with new weariness."
John Rust

What we do with our money plays a large part in determining the quality of our life! Money can add value to our life and the lives of others. It can simplify our life or make it a lot more complicated and stressful. I recommend a frugal lifestyle that keeps a close eye on spending money economically and wisely. I'm not talking about being cheap, not spending any money and never paying our fair share. I've listed ways in which I feel money is not spent wisely, such as on really big homes and expensive cars.

As the size of your home increases so will the cost of utilities, repairs and the amount of furniture and curtains needed. How big a house do you really need? Are the increased costs and extra work associated with a big house worth it?

Second homes can also add stress and complexity to our life. Vacation homes need a lot of care, repairs and security. They also may limit your vacation choices. Is it worth it? Sometimes the answer is yes. The benefits of family time together and escape from home pressures may far outweigh any extra time, money and commitment.

The important point to consider is simplicity and flexibility as highly held values that actually improve our life. If at all possible, rent second homes, boats, planes, expensive sports cars and other large purchases before you buy. Don't buy anything on the spur of the moment while on vacation. Carefully consider each of your major purchases before making them to see if they are wise, and if they add time, simplicity and value to your life and others.

"Just living isn't enough, said the butterfly. One must also have freedom, sunshine and a little flower."
Hans Christian Andersen

Money spent wisely can give you the freedom to pursue your passions, your mission and your health, and it can buy you time with friends and family, all of which will increase your happiness. Spend your money on things that support your happiness—experiences, relationships, family, health, hobbies and helping others.

Follow Solomon's advice to enjoy the fruits of your labor. In my own life, I have invested in extensive travel with my family. During the past 15 years, my wife and I have visited all seven continents and taken the family along on many of our trips. These trips have created great memories for all of our family, which are priceless.

This picture of our family was taken at a hippo pool on our camping trip into the Serengeti. You can see hippopotamuses and crocodiles in the pool behind us. We may have been too close to the edge!

On one trip to Africa, we took all four boys and two of their fiancées with us for two weeks camping in the Serengeti. Because lions often came to camp, we were not to go outside our tents at night. One night after dark, our guide and our rifle-armed guard went out with me to the boy's tents. I scratched on the tents and growled like a lion in an attempt to scare them. This worked pretty well on Sigrid, Dan's fiancée. She woke up my son, Dan, and said, "I think there is a lion outside!" Dan listened for a minute and said, "I think it might be my dad." He was used to my jokes.

After dinner one night, my son Paul snuck off and hid under my cot, and then jumped out just as I was going to bed. It was pitch black and I must admit I screamed and jumped several feet into the air. After all, there really were lots of dangerous animals around!

On another trip to Rwanda, I climbed to 10,000 feet near the top of a volcano to see the mountain gorillas. There are only about 400 of them left in the world, and none in captivity. It is a spectacular sight to come across a troop of 25 mountain gorillas feeding in a high altitude rain forest. The climb was very difficult, but worth the effort. After watching for a while, I began photographing a young male silverback. When I asked the guide, "Is this the aggressive one?" he answered, "Yes!" A moment later, the 425-pound male silverback gorilla charged me. I assumed it was either a fake charge or that he would turn to the side. Wrong! He ran right over the top of me! Fortunately, we were in almost waist high brush, and I fell backwards into it. The sun was blocked out for an instant. I felt just two medium hard thumps on my chest. Physically, I wasn't harmed. But momentarily, my psyche was severely damaged. Our driver said he had been coming to this area for over 20 years and never known this to happen. It certainly created a memory (maybe a nightmare?) for me that is priceless now that I'm back home alive and several years have passed.

*This 425-pound silverback gorilla charged and ran over the top of me,
creating a great memory (nightmare?) for my family and me.*

We have many interesting and exciting stories from our travels.
Spending money to travel has been a wonderful investment that
paid its dividends in memories. You might also want to consider
investing in memories as well as in money. Travel to other countries
can benefit others as well as ourselves. We usually brought along
gifts for the people in poorer countries. As mentioned previously,
I brought dental instruments and gave a short lecture at the dental
school in Nairobi, Kenya. We also brought pencils, deflated soccer
balls and hand pumps to inflate them for the schools.

We learned a lot from our hosts. In Kenya, we spent considerable time with the Masai tribe. One of our guides had
visited Los Angeles. He said it seemed like the streets were

paved with gold and that it would take hundreds of years for his country to catch up. When he asked me if the people there appreciate it, I was embarrassed to answer, no. Our experience in Kenya especially taught me to spend more time appreciating what I have. Albert Schweitzer may have learned this from his time in Africa when he said, "Gratitude is the secret to life."

This kind of travel may be beyond the budget of many people. But since travel was a priority for us, we sacrificed other things to budget and plan for one major trip each year. If you want to travel, you can. If you shop carefully, you will be surprised how inexpensively you can travel to many places throughout the world. Saint Augustine, who lived in a time when travel was certainly more travail than anything else, captured it perfectly when he said, "The world is a book and those who do not travel read only a page."

Travel with my family was my passion. Another passion of mine is tennis. I play tennis two or three times a week. I usually play with my wife and three of my sons who share my passion. This hobby, like my passion for travel, is an investment in time with family and great memories. On a recent Father's Day, three of my sons and I played doubles together. This was extremely enjoyable to combine a hobby with great family time.

Determine what brings you enjoyment and spend your money on it. My only caveat, and Solomon's, is that you spend it wisely. Hobbies like flying or boating can be so outrageously expensive that they become unreasonable and a drain on the family budget. Hobbies can also take you away from your family too often, like golfing and fishing, sometimes to the point that your family is neglected and your relationships fall apart. These hobbies can be fine if they are shared and supported by your family, and you can include your family in them at least some of the time.

How do I want to appreciate and enjoy my money wisely?

What ideas about enjoying money wisely do I want to implement and/or pass on as my legacy to others?

_____

_____

_____

_____

_____

_____

_____

_____

_____

_____

_____

_____

_____

CHAPTER SIX

The Simple Secrets to Financial Peace of Mind

"Choose a good reputation over great riches, for being held in high esteem is better than having silver or gold."
Proverbs 22:1

More money by itself doesn't provide financial security. Financial security is an internal state. We are so much more than just our money, our stuff and our position. These are related to our ego and can vanish in a moment. In 2009, there are best-selling books about the coming depression and best-selling books about the coming super inflation. Each book makes a compelling argument for their case.

Peter Bernstein, one of the most famous investors of the past century, writes, "We simply do not know what the future holds.

There are so many variables that it is impossible for anyone to predict the future accurately. All of that talk on CNBC is just that, talk. It's a lot of chatter signifying nothing. It will be a lot better for your finances and your peace of mind to not watch it."

On one day, July 7, 2009, I read two opposite stories on what to invest in now. In the *Wall Street Journal,* Jeremy Siegel, a professor of finance at the University Of Pennsylvania's Wharton School contended stocks are due to tower over bonds again. "The next five years will see stocks returning 7% post-inflation annually." On the same day I received the July 13 issue of *Forbes,* which had a lead article which said "If you want to avoid getting burned buying into the latest asset bubble, dump stocks, buy bonds."

> **WORRIED ABOUT THE ECONOMY?**
>
> You are not alone. A poll conducted by the National Sleep Foundation in March 2009, found that one third of Americans are losing sleep over the state of the economy.

"People can never predict when hard times might come. Like fish in a net or birds in a snare, people are often caught by sudden tragedy."
Ecclesiastes 9:12

When even the best don't know what the future holds and we get conflicting advice daily, how can one possibly have financial peace of mind? I struggled with this question and came up with the following definition of financial peace of mind. It works for me and I frequently need to remind myself of it. I hope it will help you.

> ### THREE SIMPLE SECRETS TO FINANCIAL PEACE OF MIND:
> 1. The confidence that we have the ability to figure out for ourselves how to **make more** money than we spend **or spend less** than we make.
> 2. **Be grateful** for and make the best of however much or little money we have.
> 3. **Don't participate** in the money myth.

Again Solomon thought of the second secret before I did.

"Enjoy what you have rather than desiring what you don't have."
Ecclesiastes 6:9

T. Harv Eker talks about how to apply these simple secrets in his book, *Secrets of the Millionaire Mind*, in which he writes, "Training and managing your own mind is the most important skill you could ever own, in terms of both happiness and success. You can choose your thoughts. You have the natural ability to cancel any thought that is not supporting you, at any time. You can install self-empowering thoughts simply by choosing to focus on them."

THE MONEY MYTH

My good friend, Dr. David Kagan, sent me this about how he handles and achieves financial peace of mind. He wrote, "We can never accurately predict the future number of buyers to sellers of anything. Money is not lost; it was never there! Money cannot be created nor destroyed, (except by the mint!), just the value that it represents to society."

It all goes back to basic supply and demand. The same overexuberance and crashing of the stock market, the bursting of the tech stock bubble, the crashing of the real estate market and the crash of oil and commodities are all based on irrational sentiment swings in the basic equation of supply and demand.

We cannot possibly control nor predict the zillions of intricacies which factor into what causes and influences the often-tremendous daily fluctuations in the speculation on supply and demand. It would certainly be presumptuous of us to think we would be smart enough (over a long period of time) to accurately predict what is going to happen and therefore bet on the future price of anything. It's also nearly impossible to predict the exact time when we are going to need the money.

There are just three keys in regards to being successful when it comes to money.

- Figure out who you want to be and what you want to do and the size of your contribution to society, life and humanity as a whole. What are you going to do to make other lives better, easier, more fun and enjoyable, more joyful, helpful, enthusiastic, optimistic, educated or whatever your passion and talents allow.

- The exchange of value for money that you earn, which will be in direct proportion to the size of your contribution to the world, from providing your unique talents and gifts to others, should never be put at risk, betting on some future ratio of the number of buyers to sellers of anything. Some should be spent and some should be saved in a vehicle, which is not subject to loss.

- Don't watch the news!

The money myth is a game, a fallacy and a façade that is pushed on us by this massive industry, which, on a daily basis, plays with and on our emotions. Stockbrokers, magazines and TV networks are the only ones who profit from the fluctuation, tactics and constant hyped-up 24/7 news tickers fooling us. They steal away our precious focus and attention from what is really important in our lives, which are our family, creations of value and contribution to our fellow man and posterity.

My friend concludes brilliantly with what I have added as the third secret to financial peace of mind when he wrote,

"Don't be fooled by this money myth anymore and simply **choose not to participate** *in it."*

Very wise advice, indeed!

To summarize, for financial peace of mind, make more or spend less, be grateful and ignore the money myth.

No book on money would be complete without quoting Napoleon Hill's 1960 classic, *Think and Grow Rich*. In it, Hill reveals what he calls secrets to growing rich including, "Whatever the mind of man can conceive and believe it can achieve," and the inspiring, "Every adversity, every failure and every heartache carries with it the seed of an equivalent or greater benefit." One of the first books to call attention to this power of thought was the classic *As a Man Thinketh* by James Allen published in 1902, which stated, "All that you achieve and all that you fail to achieve is the direct result of your own thoughts." These men intuitively discovered what modern mental health professionals like Aaron Beck and Albert Ellis have given scientific credibility, what is now called cognitive thinking.

When I have fearful financial thoughts, I substitute them with thoughts like my definition of financial peace of mind, Napoleon Hill's inspiring words and remembering the money myth. Sometimes, I summarize it by telling myself simply, "I have enough and I can handle this. I have before."

The next time your mind starts going nuts over money, cancel those negative thoughts and install your own positive, empowering ones. If you wish, create your own financial peace of mind statement below:

_____

_____

_____

_____

How Much Is Enough?

"Don't weary yourself trying to get rich. For riches can disappear as though they had the wings of a bird!"
Proverbs 23:4, 5

Wealth is like health in many ways. We don't appreciate it and we take it for granted until we are sick. We generally don't appreciate our money until we don't have it. We do know that lack of money at a certain point can definitely increase our misery! Witness all the moaning and groaning during our current economic difficulty.

ENOUGH?

John Bogle, the founder of the Vanguard Mutual Fund Group, tells the following story in the introduction to his book, *Enough*, "At a party given by a billionaire, Kurt Vonnegut informs his pal, Joseph Heller, that their host, a hedge fund manager, had made more money in a single day than Heller had earned from his wildly popular novel *Catch-22* over its whole history. Heller responds, 'Yes, but I have something he will never have…enough.'" For a critical element of our society, Bogle says, "Including many of the wealthiest and most powerful among us, there seems to be no limit today on what enough entails."

It's foolish to think that money is not important in our life, but even more foolish to emphasize it over all other values and not to know how much is enough. This important question is a personal one, and depends on our life goals for our money and our circumstances. For some, in the current economic climate, it might be just enough for food and shelter. For my wife and me, enough was when we reached financial independence. If you want to leave a large inheritance or a large amount to charity then financial independence would not be enough.

Vicki Robin's and Joe Dominguez's excellent book, *Your Money or Your Life,* opens with these thought provoking questions: "Your money or your life! If someone thrust a gun in your ribs and said that, what would you do? Most of us would turn over our wallets. The threat works because we value our lives more than we value our money."

Or do we?

Comedian Jack Benny played the tightwad in his shows and had a great story about this. He was accosted at gunpoint on the street and asked "Your money or your life!" He did not answer. The thief asked again, "Didn't you hear me? Your money or your life!" Jack paused and then answered, "I'm thinking, I'm thinking."

The important point is to achieve balance in our lives, enjoy the journey and not use up all our life's energy in the blind pursuit of money. Laura Nash in her book, *Just Enough*, points out, "If you don't know what you really seek and why, you'll never be able to appreciate what you get. Nothing will ever be enough!" We'll spend our life on a treadmill. As the Bible points out, "What does it profit a person to gain the world and lose one's soul?" Our achievements must resonate with our own values and beliefs.

The Frogs Who Wanted a King

Again, we can learn from the ancient wisdom in Aesop's fable about the frogs who wanted a king. Disturbed at their own lawless condition, the frogs asked the god Zeus to provide them a king. Perceiving their simplicity, Zeus dropped a log of wood into the frog's pool. It wasn't long before the frogs became dissatisfied with their king and begged Zeus for a new ruler. Exasperated, Zeus sent the frogs a stork who gobbled them all up.

The moral: Know when to leave well enough alone or know how much is enough!

Knowing how much is enough is one of the most important questions we face in determining the quality of our life. This decision has to be made at both a financial and emotional level. Remember, if we have enough, we are rich no matter what the amount! Conversely, if we don't have enough, we are poor no matter how much money we have.

Solomon nails it again in Ecclesiastes 5:10, "Those who love money will never have enough. How absurd to think that wealth brings true happiness! The more you have, the more people come to help you spend it."

**Think about it. Do you have enough
money? Do you have enough love?**

_____

_____

_____

How much is enough for you?

_____

_____

_____

I'm all for having more money as long as we don't let it consume us, and if we use it wisely. Human history makes it clear; more money rarely brings financial security. There is no amount of money that some financial disaster cannot take away. There is always a little doubt. Millions of people can attest to this. Two wealthy men actually committed suicide after losing money and reputation in the Madoff scheme. Another prominent case in point is the German businessman, Adolf Merckle. Merckle had a net worth of $9.2 billion. Gross revenues from his business were $30 billion per year. His business encountered trouble and he lost much, but not all, of his wealth. He committed suicide by throwing himself in front of a train. The suicide note he left behind reportedly said simply, "I'm sorry." He couldn't come to terms with losing the empire, which was going to be his legacy to his family. He felt that without all that money he had accumulated, he didn't have enough and was nothing. What a tragedy! In addition to coping with the loss of their father, his family was left with major financial problems. What is his legacy now? Did he finish well?

WHAT ABOUT A SEVERE RECESSION?

"If you fail under pressure, your strength is not very great."
Proverbs 24:10

"It was the best of times, it was the worst of times, it was the age of wisdom, it was the age of foolishness, it was the spring of hope, it was the winter of despair." So begins Charles Dickens' *A Tale of Two Cities*, a fascinating epic written in 1859, which is worth contemplating today.

Which is it? How we see our circumstances really is our choice isn't it? Some would say this all sounds good on paper, but what about the tough times we're facing today? Financial intelligence is never more important than in tough times! In good times, almost anything works.

We wouldn't be human if we weren't concerned about what's going on economically. We are definitely facing some financially difficult times. However, tough times never last, but tough people do. Again, things can't go on forever. The stock market

> ### LOVE LIFE, NOT STUFF
> Leo Babauta, author of the *The Power of Less*, writes in his terrific blog, "Zen Habits: Love Life, Not Stuff," that at the end of this short life, you'll look back and remember your experiences, the people you loved and who loved you, the things you did and didn't do, not the stuff you had. This economic downturn helps us to refocus on the things that truly matter.

won't keep going down forever and neither will real estate, just like it couldn't keep going up forever.

Remember that our parents and grandparents survived The Great Depression, which essentially lasted for 12 years from 1929 to the beginning of the Second World War in 1941. The Dow Jones Industrial Average dropped 89% and did not recover to the pre-1929 levels until November 23, 1954. Almost half of all homes went into foreclosure, and unemployment reached 25% with no unemployment insurance available.

That generation also lived through several of the worst wars in history. My father was captured by the Germans in the Battle of the

Bulge and spent six days being transported in a train car with little food or water. Our parents and grandparents survived these hard times pretty well and so will we. If we compare ourselves to those in most other countries, we are in considerably better shape. Ask yourself, where would you like to go that's better?

In the book, *Super Freakonomics,* the authors point out that:

"It is a fact of life that people love to complain, particularly about how terrible the modern world is compared with the past. They are nearly always wrong. On just about any dimension you can think of—warfare, crime, income, education, transportation, worker safety, health—the 21st century is far more hospitable to the average human than any earlier time. For one example, consider deaths in childbirth. Just 100 years ago, the rate was *more than 50 times* higher."

Turn Problems Into Opportunities

"The best thing for being sad," replied Merlin, "is to learn something.
That's the only thing that never fails. That is the only thing which
the mind can never exhaust, never alienate, never be tortured
by, never fear or distrust, and never dream of regretting."
T. H. White, *The Sword in the Stone*

This economic downturn is an important opportunity to learn. In my own case, I learned that I should have had more money in bonds at my age. I was more concerned about inflation and missing the upside as stocks went up than about the possibility of loss. It also helped me learn that I don't need as much money as I thought I did to be happy, satisfied and peaceful. An economic downturn can give us time to reflect and help us reassess our values. It allows us to focus more on relationships and less on accumulating stuff. I think it reminded us all of the dangers of conspicuous consumption and freefall greed.

Again, we can learn from the ancient wisdom of the apostle Paul in his letter to Timothy: "For the love of money is the root of all kinds of evil." Notice that Paul says the "love" of money. Money is necessary. The "love of money" is more like greed. After years of conspicuous consumption, Americans have been jolted into realizing we must get back to basic values and live within our means. Michael Douglas won the Academy Award for best actor in the 1987 movie *Wall Street*. In it he says, "Greed is good." I think we have learned over the past several decades that it isn't! This is a hugely important lesson for our generation and for future generations.

What can you learn from economic downturns?

_____

_____

_____

_____

_____

When things go wrong, instead of calling them *mess*takes, we can welcome them as "learning opportunities." Ronald Reagan was famous for his attitude toward adversity, "There must be a pony under that pile of manure somewhere." One of the keys to enlightened living is to see the opportunity in each problem, in other words, to turn lemons into lemonade.

Turn Lemons into Lemonade

Houses are now much more affordable for young people at a time when housing was becoming unaffordable. The thousands of homes that have been lost have mostly been found by someone else at a lower price. There is much less pressure to keep up with the Joneses. In addition, stock prices became more reasonable, making the upside potential greater than when stocks were selling for 30 times earnings or more. The economic downturn exposed many scams and Ponzi schemes before they could steal even more money from us. As Warren Buffett said, "When the water goes down, it exposes those who are in the water without any clothes on."

Excessive compensation for senior executives is being brought under control to more accurately represent their actual results. Prices on many items are also much less. In our own case, my wife and I went on two cruises that cost less than half as much as they did a year ago!

What opportunities can you see in economic downturns?

_____

_____

_____

_____

_____

BUT WHEN WILL I GET MY MONEY BACK?

It's not as bad as you think! If you had a 30% loss on a $300,000 portfolio, you can save $10,000 a year and, with an 8% return, recover your loss in three years. If you had a 30% loss on a $500,000 portfolio, you can save $15,000 per year and, with an 8% return, recover your loss in only three years. So the answer to the question, when will you get your money back, is: in three years! In the previous illustrations, even with only a 3 to 4% return, you will have your money back in five years.

Financial health, as we've discussed throughout this book, is only one area of life. Many of us make the big *mess*take of focusing almost all of our time, energy and self-esteem in this area, often losing our health, relationships and, ultimately, our happiness in the process.

"Even if you win the rat race, you're still a rat!"
Lily Tomlin

It's important to remember during the times we have less money that when we had more money, we were still stressed. Sales for antidepressants and anti-anxiety medications increased exponentially during the last decade before the recession. Rather than relieving stress, having lots of money has the potential to make life more stressful. Money is not a protection from anything, really, except maybe creditors.

Finally, to keep things in perspective, it's important to remember how much money you'll leave when you die…all of it! When he heard this, the famous comedian Bob Hope, said, "Then, I'm not going!" Unfortunately, I don't think we have a choice.

CHAPTER SEVEN

Finishing Well by Living a *Highly Successful Life*

"Finishing is better than starting."
Ecclesiastes 7:8

Equally as important as financial health is spiritual, mental, physical and relationship health. We still have our purpose to help others. We can still choose to be happy, since happiness is only one thought away. If we take care of ourselves, we still have our health. And we can still have great relationships with our significant others and friends. And, our circumstances are much better than most since we live in the United States! So for me, living well and finishing well is considerably more than just financial health.

It is living each day *a highly successful life* as I defined it in the introduction, "Going the extra mile to be wind on people's back through great relationships, while feeling happy, satisfied and peaceful, healthy, energetic and financially free." This is how I want to live each day and the legacy that I hope to leave.

I discussed in the introduction the "Five Really Big *Mess*takes." We make these *mess*takes in the five key areas that I consider part of living *a highly successful life*. These areas are: spiritual health, mental health, physical health, relationship health and financial health.

I mentioned in the beginning of the book the challenges of sorting out conflicting advice about finances. This is equally true, if not more so, about living *a highly successful life*. Many believe that if you have spiritual health that is all you need to live *a highly successful life*. Others believe that if you're happy, then you've lived *a highly successful life*. Some say if you're energetic and take good care of your body, you are highly successful. Some believe that if you have great relationships, you have all you need for *a highly successful life*. Others believe that if you've been financially successful then you've lived *a highly successful life*.

There is a grain of truth in all of these positions. For me, having a semblance of balance in all of these areas is how I define *a highly successful life*. As I said about finances, study different points of view and then decide for yourself what works. There are probably hundreds if not thousands of different philosophies for living *a highly successful life*. This is just my version.

How to Avoid the Five Really Big *MESS*TAKES

In my opinion, you can't avoid all *mess*takes, but you can get a lot better at it and also feel super more of the time. As I mentioned in the introduction when I discussed implementation, measurement always improves performance. I measure myself each night on how I did in each area by writing out the easy to remember acronym: SUPER.

The S stands for spiritual health, the U stands for feeling up/ mental health, the P stands for prosperity/financial health, the E stands for energy, the essential measure of physical health, and the R stands for relationship health.

I then grade myself in each area. For me an eight is an A in that area. For example, in the spiritual area, if I focused on my mission to help others at least some of the time that day, I might give myself an eight. I would give myself a ten if, like Mother Teresa, I spent my entire day helping others. I don't ask myself to be perfect in each area. In mental health, I don't require myself to be ecstatically happy all day, just basically happy overall. That would earn an 8.

In the illustration below, I gave myself a 6 in feeling up/mental health, so I would want to start working to improve that area. I gave myself a 5 on physical health/exercise so I definitely would want to look at what was going on in my physical health that day. What would I need to do tomorrow to increase my energy, get enough exercise and eat less calories than I burn? It looks like this:

S-U-P-E-R
7-6-7-5-7

If I give myself a 7, that's a B and that's okay with me. However, if I give myself a 6 or (God forbid) below a 6, then I make a goal to work on this the next day.

So there you have it; my foolproof strategy for living *a highly successful life* and feeling SUPER all the time!

Just kidding. It does not exist. As I mentioned when I discussed financial peace of mind, I suggest we also give up searching for the

Holy Grail of life management. It's absolutely human to not feel SUPER some of the time and to struggle with keeping all five areas of our life on course.

If you earn an 8 or higher in each area, I'll call you Superman or Superwoman. A worthy goal!

By measuring myself each day, I'm able to stay basically on course to live *a highly successful life* and feel SUPER most of the time. To receive your free "Success Scorecard" and begin to feel SUPER more of the time, go to www.lifesbig*mess*takes.com and start using it tonight.

GRATITUDE

"I cannot tell you anything that, in a few minutes, will tell you how to be rich. But I can tell you how to feel rich, which is far better, let me tell you firsthand, than being rich. Be grateful. It's the only totally reliable get-rich-quick scheme."
Ben Stein

There's one other thing that I do at the end of the day that's made an immense difference in the quality of my life. I write down in my journal, first, all the people I'm grateful for in my life and second all the things for which I am grateful. I list at least four unique things that happened that day for which I'm grateful. I don't stop until I get at least four which seldom takes very long.

Robert Emmons, PhD, illustrates the benefits of this exercise in his terrific book: *Thanks! How the New Science of Gratitude Can Make You Happier.* Dr. Emmons cites his own research to prove that people who regularly practice grateful thinking can increase their happiness "set point" by as much as 25%, and sustain this increase over several months. He also cites research that shows that keeping a gratitude journal for as little as three weeks can result in better sleep and more energy.

Try this. It certainly has worked for me.

I think that Nobel Peace Prize winner, Albert Schweitzer, discovered something when he said, "Gratitude is the secret to life!"

Write out–what are you grateful for?
You'll feel better immediately.

_____

_____

_____

_____

_____

_____

_____

Rediscovering the Five Great Secrets
to Living *A HIGHLY SUCCESSFUL LIFE*

We've now come full circle from the beginning of the book when I told you my initial intention was to write about all five areas of our life, and then decided to focus on financial health because of the current economic crisis. My book writing coach, Yolanda, wants to know the "rest of the story" so that she and others can act appropriately in each area.

Here's how I correct myself after making each of the Five Big *Mess*takes for a score of less than 8.

I remind myself of my definition of *a highly successful life* is going the extra mile to be "wind on people's back" through great relationships, while feeling happy, satisfied and peaceful, healthy and energetic and financially free.

Here are the "secrets" to living this highly successful life in more detail as I have rediscovered them, and the standard that I set for an 8 in each area. Figure out for yourself what your secrets are to living your highly successful life, and what your standard is in each area. Again, I found that Solomon and others had discovered these so-called "secrets" way before I did.

Spiritual health: *The Why*–My mission is to go the extra mile to be wind on people's backs by relieving all the suffering that I can and increasing all the happiness that I can. This is not too different from Scott Peck's definition of love in his best-selling book, *The Road Less Traveled*. He defines love thus, "The will to extend one's self for the purpose of nurturing one's own or another's spiritual growth." So spiritual health is really about extending love!

I don't think anybody has said this better than the apostle Paul 2,000 years ago:

"Love never ends; as for prophecies, they will pass away; as for tongues, they will cease; as for knowledge, it will pass away. So faith, hope, love abide, these three, but the greatest of these is love."
Corinthians 13:8, 13

As I said in the introduction, when I quote Solomon and Paul, I'm not necessarily referring to any specific religious faith. I'm quoting them for their timeless and inspired wisdom. I do believe a religious belief usually greatly enhances spiritual health. As I also said before, spiritual health is the most critical health of all and empowers all the others.

Psychiatrist Victor Frankl, the author of *Man's Search for Meaning*, has said that, "Those who have a why to live can bear with almost any how." He used his desire to write about his experiences that helped him survive, despite incredibly long odds, for three years in Nazi concentration camps.

My father used the same motivation to survive after being captured by the Germans in the Battle of the Bulge. He was placed in a closed railroad car for six days with little food and water. He survived by licking frozen water on the edge of the car. He then spent 99 days in a prison camp with little food and went from 160 pounds to 100 pounds. When he and his fellow soldiers were being marched to the rear, some of the soldiers would just give up and were often shot. He was able to keep motivated and keep going because of a picture of my mother and myself that he carried with him. He would even show the picture to the guards in the camp and they were sometimes nicer to him. Thankfully, for my family and me, he had a "why" to live!

This is a copy of the photo of my parents and myself that my
dad carried during World War II to help him survive.

My motivation for writing this book was to fulfill what I perceived as my mission after my heart incident, to share what I had learned (extending a small gift of love) about finances and life to make the biggest possible contribution to the most people. I suggest always looking for a "why" or mission for almost everything that you do. This may truly be "the secret to life!"

Mental health: *The Will*–I will remember to manage my thoughts, to stop my negative thought attacks, and welcome problems as opportunities for learning and growth. For the most part, I will choose happy, satisfied and peaceful thoughts. Solomon knew the importance of happiness 3,000 years ago.

"A cheerful heart is good medicine, but a
broken spirit saps a person's strength."
Proverbs 17:22

Massive scientific literature now indicates that there are many intentional activities that can increase our so-called genetic "set point" for happiness. Contrary to what you may have heard, you <u>can</u> successfully pursue happiness. In fact, Dr. Sonja Lyubomirsky, a University of California professor of psychology, calls this "the most rewarding 'work' you'll ever do." She has outlined how to do this in her book *The How of Happiness, A Scientific Approach to Getting the Life You Want* and on a terrific iPhone app called LiveHappy. In addition to the gratitude journal, she suggests practicing optimism, remembering and savoring happy life moments, nurturing relationships, setting goals and striving to achieve them and doing acts of kindness.

Physical health: *The Energy*–I will exercise regularly, get proper rest, eat right and eat fewer calories than I burn. You can't make a contribution without energy to do it.

"Don't let the sparkle and smooth taste of wine deceive you. For in
the end it bites like a poisonous serpent; it stings like a viper."
Proverbs 23: 31, 32

Relationship health: *The Way*–I will remember that we are all connected so that I love people despite the reasons they give me not to love them, and ignore and forgive their bad behavior because I understand them as suffering and calling for love as I am.

"Disregarding another person's faults preserves love."
Proverbs 17:9

I will then proactively fill their buckets with random acts of kindness, love and positive recognition. This statement also applies to how we treat ourselves since we can be our own worst critic. I believe the quality of our lives is directly proportional to the quality of our relationships with family, friends, co-workers and clients.

"Kind words are like honey—sweet to the
soul and healthy for the body."
Proverbs 16:24

Financial health: *The Means*–I will have the confidence that I have the ability to figure out for myself how to make more money than I spend, or spend less than I make, to be grateful and enjoy what I have, and make the best of it, however much or little I do have. I will spend it wisely on things that add value to my life and to others. Remember, even Mother Teresa needed money to do her good work.

"Wisdom or money can get you almost anything, but it's
important to know that only wisdom can save your life."
Ecclesiastes 7:12

Many large books have been written about the first four areas, and I may eventually write some small ones, if my wife will support me after she and I recover from this project. I've listed some of these more detailed sources in the bibliography.

Having set this very high standard for my life, I hasten to repeat that, I am a fellow traveler with you, and I often have days and moments where I veer off this path. It has been said that we use the stars for navigation, but we don't expect to reach them.

"There's not a single person in all the earth
who is always good and never sins."
Ecclesiastes 7:20

Often I forget to go the extra mile to be helpful to others and instead focus on my own needs. Sometimes this is appropriate. Not all of my relationships are great. Unfortunately, this too is part of life. I have low moods. In fact, when I got a little irritable as the deadline approached on this book, my team recommended that I reread my own book! Unfortunately, they were right!

"If you listen to constructive criticism, you
will be at home among the wise."
Proverbs 15:31

Some health problems are genetic or heaven sent and unavoidable. My heart problem might qualify for this. I seldom wake up in the morning feeling energetic. When we are bombarded with fear and greed stories daily, I struggle with peace, especially about money. Even with all that I have accomplished financially, I still have the occasional depression-era mentality and don't feel financially free.

When this happens to me, I remind myself of the fourth agreement from Don Miguel Ruiz's book, *The Four Agreements*, which is: always do your best. He writes, "Your best is going to change from moment to moment; it will be different when you are healthy as opposed to when you are sick. Under any circumstance, simply do your best and you will avoid self judgment, self abuse and regret."

Remembering this agreement helps me face problems. So be gracious with yourself when you're less-than-perfect and simply do your best! I believe I can say that on most days, I did my best. Just as I believe that in writing this book, "I simply did my best."

After reading this book, what is your definition of *a highly successful life?*

_____

_____

_____

_____

Which of the areas discussed do you want to work on to be able to live it?

_____

_____

_____

_____

Ideas for achieving financial peace of mind that I want to implement and/or pass on to others as my legacy.

_____

_____

_____

_____

WILL YOU BE ADMITTED TO HEAVEN?

"The idea is not to get rich quickly, but to have a rich life."
Warren Buffet

In the movie, *The Bucket List*, Morgan Freeman tells Jack Nicholson the ancient Egyptians believed that when your soul gets to heaven, the gods ask you two questions. Your answers determined whether you were admitted or not. The first question was: Have you found joy in your life? The second was: Has your life brought joy to others? Nicholson answers yes to the first question, but defers to others for the answer to the second question. Morgan Freeman counters, "I'm asking you!"

As one test for finishing well, these seem like good questions to ask. At least for today, I feel like I can answer yes to both of these questions.

How would you answer these questions? "I'm asking you!"

1. Have you found joy in your life? Y N

2. Has your life brought joy to others? Y N

**If you answered no to either question, what is
your plan to change the answer to yes?**

_____

_____

_____

_____

This book is a summary of my thoughts about money and life that I want to continue to use and leave as a legacy to my children, grandchildren, and others. It is well researched and thought out, but I don't have quite the confidence of Charles Barkley who titled his book, *I May be Wrong But I Doubt It.*

Solomon points this out in Proverbs 3:7, "Don't be impressed with your own wisdom." He then adds in Proverbs 16:18, "Pride goes before destruction and haughtiness before a fall."

Check out my ideas with others and see if they are right for you. If what you are doing is working, don't change it. As Solomon says in Proverbs 18:17, "Any story sounds true until someone sets the record straight."

I hope you find these ideas helpful and that, like Scrooge who lived well and finished well after Marley's warning, you will live well and finish well with the help of this book.

Kendrick Mercer has a quote in his brilliant book, *Time and Money*, "Life is a process, not an end; if you don't enjoy the process, you'll hate the end!"

What thoughts about money and life would you like to leave as a legacy for your children, grandchildren and others? Summarize the ideas you have written down from previous chapters, and if you wish, use the space below to add more ideas and modify mine as you feel appropriate. Pass these ideas on to your family and friends, and give or tell people about this book as part of your legacy of joy and hope for present and future generations.

Good luck with your writing and with your commitment to reaching financial health, living well, leaving a positive legacy, and finishing well!

_____

_____

_____

_____

_____

_____

_____

_____

_____

Like the young man described in the introduction who was
helping the starfish, my goal for this book is to make a difference
for you. My hope is that you will be able to create
some value from my "small gift of love."

Conclusion—The Paradox of Life

Some of you may disagree with some, or even many of the principles and opinions I express in this book, and some may even be upset. That's fine. As one of my favorite philosophers and comedian Groucho Marx said, "Well, those are my principles, if you don't like them, I have others." And, as one of my other favorite philosophers, baseball great Yogi Berra said, "I really didn't say everything I said!" This will be difficult for me to pull off since I am essentially quoting myself, but I'm using it anyway.

I hope your review of my book will be better than the one Groucho wrote for S. J. Perelman's book *Monkey Business*, in which he wrote, "From the moment I picked up your book until I laid it down, I was convulsed with laughter. Someday I intend reading it."

Susanna McMahon in her brilliant book, *The Portable Therapist*, writes, "Paradoxically we are taught that we have to defend and protect ourselves, that we cannot appear vulnerable or others will take advantage of us. Actually, the opposite occurs.

The easiest and fastest way to understand paradox is through the use of humor. Laugh at yourself and with others. Do not take anything seriously. It is all a game and we are all players. The best we can be occurs when we let go and have fun and play the game spontaneously. This is the paradox of life." Sounds good to me!

"So I concluded that there is nothing better for people than to be happy and to enjoy themselves as long as they can."
Ecclesiastes 3:12

Rediscover Solomon's advice about life and money, don't make the big *mess*take I made for a lot of my life—taking things too seriously. Lighten up about money and life. Have fun and enjoy a prosperous and *highly successful life*—as you define it.

THE BEGINNING...

Congratulations on making it to the end of this book. You're now at the beginning of a new more helpful, happier, healthier, wealthier, and wiser financial and personal life.

Since word of mouth is the best advertisement, if you found this book helpful and you feel comfortable doing so, please pass it on to as many people as possible. Its purpose is to make the biggest possible contribution to the most people by leaving a legacy of joy and hope for present and future generations.

ABOUT THE AUTHOR

Dr. Tom McCawley earned his dental degree from the University of Illinois College of Dentistry and a Certificate of Advanced Graduate Study in Periodontics from the Boston University School of Graduate Dentistry. From 1969 to 1972, he served in the U.S. Army as Chief of Periodontics at the Baumholder, Germany Dental Center. Dr. McCawley has practiced periodontics in Fort Lauderdale since 1972. He is past president of the Florida Academy of Dental Practice Administration and the Florida Society of Periodontists. He is a Fellow of the American College of Dentists and has been a member of the Board of Directors for the North American Society of Periodontics since 1990 and an adjunct clinical assistant professor at Nova Southeastern University College of Dental Medicine since 1997.

- Dr. McCawley has studied and lectured on the subjects of life management, financial management and dental practice management for over 30 years.

- He has lectured more than 100 times on these subjects including at the University of Southern California, the University of Florida and the Nova Southeastern University College of Dental Medicine, as well as to local and state dental groups.

- He presents this material in two separate lectures annually to the senior dental students at NSU.

- Internationally, he has presented his program to dental societies in Sydney, Australia and Cape Town, South Africa.

- He lectures annually to the periodontal graduate students at NSU on another of his interests, microbiology and the use of antibiotics to treat periodontal disease.

- He has published numerous articles in dental journals and newsletters, including a research article on lasers in the *Journal of the American Academy of Periodontology* and a review article on lasers in the *Journal of the Florida Dental Association.*

- Dr. McCawley is one of the pioneers in using lasers to treat periodontal disease. He had one of the first Nd:YAG lasers in the country in 1990. He has personally treated over 3,000 patients with laser technology and lectures frequently on new minimally invasive breakthrough laser treatments for periodontal disease.

- He is co-editor of a dental newsletter, *The PerioDontaLetter,* which mails to approximately 10,000 dentists.

Dr. McCawley challenges and grades himself at the end of each day (by his **SUPER** score) to avoid life's five really big *mess*takes, and to live fully in each of the five key areas he defines as essential to living *a highly successful life*: **spiritually** by making the biggest possible contribution to others, **mentally** by taking responsibility for a positive attitude; **physically** by staying in peak physical health and shape; by creating great **relationships**, and finally, by building

financial freedom, which enables him to contribute to others and fully enjoy his life.

He has been happily married to Brenda for 29 years and has four sons. Three of his sons are lawyers. And one is in dental school at Nova Southeastern. He has six grandchildren. All of his children and grandchildren live in Fort Lauderdale.

His hobbies are tennis and travel—and living, writing and lecturing about living *a highly successful life*, finishing well and enjoying the journey.

Sources for Additional Information

If you would like additional books to pass on as part of your legacy, please go to www.lifesbig*mess*takes.com or email us at booking@thekeynotegroup.com. Ask us about volume discounts for larger book orders.

To book Dr. McCawley for your next event please call us at 954-791-7991 or email us at booking@thekeynotegroup.com. You can also visit www.lifesbig*mess*takes to see Dr. McCawley's speaking topics, client testimonials, interviews and presentations.

His topics include "Avoiding Life's 5 Big *Mess*takes," "Avoiding Life's Big Financial *Mess*takes," and for dental professionals: "Avoiding the 10 Big Dental Practice Management *Mess*takes."

For additional information about Dr. McCawley and periodontal disease, dental implants and laser treatments, visit his office website at www.mccawleydeture.com

We would like to hear how this book has helped you in your personal or financial life. You can contact Dr. McCawley at his blog at www.lifesbig*mess*takes.com/blog. He appreciates your feedback and comments.

To receive your free "Success Scorecard" and begin to feel SUPER more of the time, go to www.lifesbig*mess*takes.com and start using it tonight.

What Others Say About Dr. McCawley's Talks and Information

"Your lecture was life changing for me. I felt so inspired by your outlook on life and feel that so many of us miss the message regarding success in life! I walked away feeling so invigorated to attempt life with entirely new meaning. Many parts of your talk brought tears to my eyes! It melted my heart in so many ways! Tom, you're such an inspiration and should share this message throughout the world!"

Lisa Heintskill, RDH, BA, MS,
PhD candidate Nova Southeastern University
Program Director at NSU's College of Dental
Medicine's North Miami Beach Campus

"Tom McCawley is the most authentic speaker I've ever heard. What you see is what you get—direct, funny, insightful and uplifting. He's exactly what dentists, newly graduated and seasoned alike, need to hear more of. Thanks Tom, for all of your advice which is at once proven and fresh."

Patrick Wahl, DMD, MBA
Owner of Office Magic
Wilmington, Delaware

"Reading this book is a potentially life changing event—setting you on your way to even greater financial health, and most importantly *a highly successful life*. A must-read book filled with practical information!"

David Kagan, DMD and Juli Kagan RDH;
Author of *Mind Your Body—Pilates for the Seated Professional*
Boca Raton, Florida

"Tom McCawley is the single most credible source of high-value practice building information. Over the years, when I turned to Tom for help, I've always come away with powerful insights that apply to all dentists who are serious about practice growth. I consider him among my most valuable resources for next level coaching information and, above all, he's easy to listen to."

Greg Stanley
Owner of Whitehall Management
Scottsdale, Arizona

"We have known Tom McCawley for many years. We had the distinct privilege to attend a live presentation of this program. The first part is chock full of marvelous practice pearls that will enrich your practice; the second portion contains a compelling message that every dentist needs to hear. It will benefit you and your family in ways you cannot imagine and may even save your life."

Bob and Marci Proebstle
Owners of Accelerated Practice Concepts
Minneapolis, Minnesota

"I loved it! You have done an incredible job and I know this book is going to be a bestseller! Easy to read, love the art, and not complicated. You said what you wanted to say in a way people will be able to read quickly. I truly wish I would have had your book when I started out. Yes, I have made big *mess*takes but lucky for me I always was able to recover. Congratulations on doing a great job! This will help many people along life's path."

Debbie E. Berdy, CEO
Contemporary Management Concepts
Alachua, Florida

Appendix

How to Find the "Normalized" Price to Earnings Ratio

The challenge is finding the "normalized" price to earnings ratio for the S&P 500 Index. Here's how: Google the Robert Shiller home page, then open the information site for his book *Irrational Exuberance*, then open the Excel file with the data set which is in the first sentence on this book site, the second tab at the bottom (figure 1.3) will show a graph of the ratio compared to long-term interest rates and the third tab (Stock Data) will show the normalized ratio figured on a monthly basis. For example, as of October 16, 2009 the normalized P/E ratio was 19.45. For comparison in 1929, it was 34 and in 2000, it was 44. In March 2009, it was 13. As you can see from this example, when this ratio gets really high usually stocks will get lower soon and when it gets low stocks have the potential to go up. Because of this "normalized" ratio's ability to indicate whether stocks are undervalued or overvalued, it's very important to know this ratio and now you know where to find it!

Bibliography

I've attempted to credit all the sources that I could remember or recover. As I quoted Solomon, there are no new ideas. Some of these ideas I came up with on my own and then discovered that others also had them. Many I borrowed from others. I've undoubtedly made a few *mess*takes. I apologize for any errors or lack of reference to any person or thing, living or dead, it is purely unintentional. The following is a partial list of my chief resources. The ones marked with an asterisk are the most valuable in my opinion. I also recommend reading *The Wall Street Journal* daily and subscribing to *Forbes* and *Money* magazines to keep up-to-date on financial matters.

Aesop's Fables. Barnes and Noble Classics. (500 BC) 2003.

Album, Mitch. *Tuesday's with Morrie: An Old Man, A Young Man and Life's Greatest Lesson*. Doubleday. 1997.

Allen, James. *As a Man Thinketh*. (1902) Penguin. 2008.

Babauta, Leo. *The Power of Less*. Hyperion. 2009.

Berra, Yogi. *The Yogi Book*. Workman Publishing. 1998.

Blue, Ron and Jeremy White. *Surviving Financial Meltdown*. Tyndale House Publishers. 2009.

*Blue, Ron and Jeremy White. *The New Master Your Money*. Moody Publishers. 2004.

Bogle, John C. *Enough*. John Wiley & Sons, Inc. 2009.

Chilton, David. *The Wealthy Barber*. (1989) Three Rivers Press. 1998.

*Clason, George S. *The Richest Man in Babylon*. (1926) Best Success Books. 2008.

*Collier, Sarner. Newsletter. www.CSANEWS.com. 2009.

*Covey, Stephen R. *The 7 Habits of Highly Effective People*. Simon and Schuster. 1990.

Dalai Lama. *The Dalai Lama's Book of Wisdom*. Thorsen's. 1999.

Dickens, Charles. *A Christmas Carol*. Ticknor and Fields. 1843.

Dickens, Charles. *David Copperfield*. Tickner and Fields. 1850.

Dickens, Charles. *A Tale of Two Cities*. Ticknor and Fields. 1859.

Eker, Harv T. *Secrets of a Millionaire Mind*. HarperCollins. 2005.

Emmons, Robert A. *Thanks! How the New Science of Gratitude Can Make You Happier*. Houghton Mifflin. 2007.

Frankl, Viktor. *Man's Search for Meaning: From Death-Camp to Existentialism*, (1946). Beacon Press. 2006.

Galbreath, John Kenneth. *A Short History of Financial Euphoria*. Viking, Penguin. 1993.

Gilbert, Daniel. *Stumbling on Happiness*. A. Knof. 2006.

Gladwell, Malcolm. *Outliers*. Little, Brown & Co. 2008.

Goodman, Steven and Andrea Leiman. *College Admissions Together: It Takes a Family*. Capital Books, 2007.

Gottman, John. *Making Marriage Work*. www.betterlifemedia.com

Graham, Benjamin and Jason Zweig. *The Intelligent Investor*. (1949) HarperCollins. 2003.

Higgins, Tim. *Pay for College Without Sacrificing Your Retirement*. Bay Tree Publishing. 2008

Hill, Napoleon. *Think and Grow Rich*. Fawcett Crest Books. 1960.

Hurley, Joseph. *Family Guide to College Savings.* Bankrate, Inc. 2009. savingforcollege.com

Kagan, Juli. *Mind your Body—Pilates for the Seated Professional.* MindBody Publishing. 2008

Kiyosaki, Robert T. *Rich Dad's Guide to Investing.* Warner Business Books. 2000.

Kiyosaki, Robert T. *Increasing your Financial IQ.* Business Plus. 2008.

Leiter, Michael and Christina Maslach. *Banishing Burnout.* John Wiley and Sons. 2005.

Levitt, Stephen D. and Stephen J. Dubner. *Super Freakonomics.* HarperCollins. 2009.

Louvish, Simon. *Coffee with Groucho.* Duncan Baird Publishers. 2007.

*Lyubomirsky, Sonja. *The How of Happiness.* Penguin Press. 2008. IPhone app LiveHappy

Maslach, Christina. *Burnout: The Cost of Caring.* Malor. 2003.

MacKay, Charles. *Extraordinary Popular Delusions and the Madness of Crowds.* (1841) Wilder Publications. 2008.

Maslow, Abraham. *Maslow on Management.* John Wiley and Sons. 1998.

Matsen, Brad. *Titanic's Last Secrets.* Hachette Book Group. 2008.

McMahon, Susanna. *The Portable Therapist.* Dell Publishing. 1992.

*Mercer, Kendrick, and Albert Goering. *Your Guide to Economic Freedom: Time and Money.* ACGPress. 2004.

Myers, L.T. *The Sinking of the Titanic.* Nimbus Publishing. 1912

Nash, Laura and Howard Stevenson. *Just Enough*. John Wiley & Sons. 2004.

Opdyke, Jeff. *Financially Ever After: The Couples Guide to Managing Money*. HarperCollins. 2009.

Orman, Suze. *The 9 Steps to Financial Freedom*. Three Rivers Press. 2006.

*Orman, Suze. *2009 Action Plan–Keeping Your Money Safe and Sound*. Spiegel & Grau. 2009

*Pankey, Lindsey D. and William J. Davis. *A Philosophy of the Practice of Dentistry*. Medical College Press. 1985.

*Peck, M. Scott. *The Road Less Traveled*. Simon & Schuster. 1978.

Porras, Jerry, et al. *Success Built to Last: Creating a Life That Matters*. Wharton School Publishing. 2006.

*Ramsey, Dave. *The Total Money Makeover*. Thomas Nelson, Inc. 2007.

Reeb, Lloyd. *From Success to Significance: When the Pursuit of Success Isn't Enough*. www.halftime.org.

*Robin, Vicki, and Joe Dominguez. *Your Money or Your Life*. Penguin Press. 2008.

Robinson, Ray. *Famous Last Words*. Workman Publishing. 2003.

*Rogers, Jim. *A Gift to My Children*. Random House. 2009.

Rubin, Gretchen. *The Happiness Project*. HarperCollins. 2009.

Ruiz, Don Miguel. *The Four Agreements*. Amber-Allen. 1997.

Schlossberg, Nancy K. *Retire Smart, Retire Happy*. APA LifeTools. 2004.

Schuller, Robert H. *Possibility Thinkers Bible: Proverbs* (1000 BC). Nelson. 1982.

Shiller, Robert. *Irrational Exuberance*. Random House. 2006.

*Sound Mind Investing Newsletter. www.soundmindinvesting. com. 2009.

Stein, Ben and Phil DeMuth. *Yes, You Can Still Retire Comfortably!* New Beginnings Press. 2005.

*The McGill Advisory Newsletter. www.BMHgroup.com. 2009.

Tuttle, Matthew. *How Harvard and Yale Beat the Market*. Wiley. 2009.

*Wilkinson, Bruce H. *The Daily Walk Bible. Proverbs* (1000 BC). New Living Translation, Tyndale House. 1997.

Zweig, Jason. *Your Money and Your Brain*. Simon & Schuster. 2007.

"But, my child, be warned: There is no end of opinions ready to be expressed. Studying them can go on forever and become very exhausting!"
Ecclesiastes 12:12

Summary of Ideas I Want to Implement–The Final Step!

When I read a book I almost always write down in the back a summary of ideas that I want to implement. This has greatly helped me to apply what I learn.

The final step is to review your goals frequently and take small steps each day. As Confucius said, "A journey of 1,000 miles begins with a single step." Divide your goals into small steps and begin! This is how I wrote this book in eight months–one small section at a time.

Use this space to write down your key goals, and then prioritize them and give them a timeline–"by when." As I stated in the beginning of the book, writing down the things that you want to implement will greatly increase your chances of implementation and that's no *mess*take!

1. _____

2. _____

3. _____

4. _____

5. _____

6. _____

7. _____

8. _____

"If you wait for perfect conditions, you will never get anything done."
Ecclesiastes 11:4

This quote helped me with my mission to write this book as doubts came frequently.

"Forget not once this journey is begun the end is certain. Doubt along the way will come and go and go to come again. Yet is the ending sure."

Epilogue, A Course in Miracles

Printed in the USA
CPSIA information can be obtained
at www.ICGtesting.com
JSHW012027140824
68134JS00033B/2916